SALES FORECASTING

PROCESS AND METHODOLOGY IN PRACTICE

PETER KARL WISEMAN

DEDICATION

I dedicate this book to the Women of my life: Iga, Gabriella and Margaret,
The Phenomena so beautifully unpredictable

Table of Contents

Acknowledgments

Margaret thank you for your help and support without which this book wouldn't be published.

Support young and talented people - part of royalties is donated to charitable organizations.

Preface

This publication does not purport to feature any complex plot, nor is it an exhaustive encyclopedia on forecasting of sales. It is intended as a concise yet complete guidebook on issues to tackle and possibly solve, analysis to conduct and methods to adopt in order to swiftly and efficiently implement or improve the sales forecasting process across any organization. Readers will find in this publication an outline of all major forecasting and forecasting quality evaluation methodologies applied in business. It helps to set up a plan and a checklist of issues that need to be followed up on, a list of people and organizational resources to be involved and actions to be taken in order to prepare and apply a professional forecasting process on par with worldwide standards.

Considering the environment in which majority of organizations operate, this publication does not make any suggestions for outsourcing any specific consulting services and/or purchasing any specialist software. The author believes that most managers are capable of implementing such measures of their own accord, and this publication is simply meant to support them so that any of their actions use the organization's resources in the most efficient manner.

Thanks to the shared experience and knowledge, this guidebook will help you avoid any initial hiccups and relatively quickly obtain the desired results. The presented issues refer not so much to the analytics and the statistical methods but rather to the process and its organization in relation to the presented methodology. This guidebook has been intended to share the good practice in the area of process organization, connecting it to the analytics area and other key areas of the organization (sales, marketing, finances, operations, strategy, etc.) so as to relatively quickly improve the forecasts and thus improve the organization's financial performance.

It is important to bear in mind that although it discusses a lot of issues, this book does not purport to be a one-stop-shop book where everyone will find exhaustive answers to any questions on forecasting. The sheer volume of such work would discourage anyone interested to quickly learn where to start and where to pay special attention. Therefore, keeping the guidebook structure will allow the readers to find references to materials which contain more detailed information on specific subjects and some chapters may be more useful than others, depending on the area of business and competences that they represent.

This publication does not cover forecasting stock exchange for reasons explained further below, however, the information presented here will definitely be useful to everyone interested in investing on stock markets.

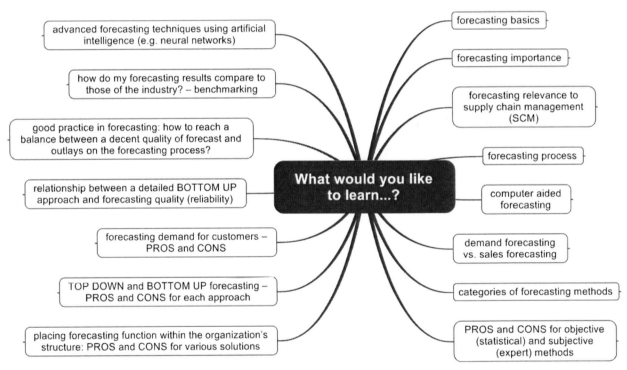

Figure 1 - Issues most often raised for discussion by participants of the sales forecasting workshops

Considering the readers' interest in this book, their business awareness and business awareness of their organizations suggests increased focus on forecasting as a major competitive edge and in many cases such focus is simply imposed by the market environment.

It is also necessary to mention the

vocabulary used in this publication. Whenever possible commonly known expressions and phrases are used as it was not the author's intention to create yet another business lingo but to discuss issues at hand in a comprehensible fashion and connect them to other publications and business areas.

At the end of this preface, please find a list of issues indicated by participants of the sales forecasting workshops as most important to them. Majority of those issues are discussed throughout this book.

1. Introduction to the Sales Forecasting

In this chapter...
- origins of forecasting in business,
- why is forecasting difficult and what are the influencing factors,
- how does forecasting success translate into business profitability.

History of forecasting

It is not this publication's intention to give readers an in depth look into origins of forecasting. It is a well-known fact that people have engaged in forecasting for thousands of years.

On the one hand, all ancient civilizations had their fortune tellers, prophets, clairvoyants, etc. Although modern times see such practices mostly as irrational, also today, perhaps even more so, we need to be able to predict the future, believe in such predictions and, what is even more important, we need to be able to influence others so that they treat such predictions seriously.

On the other hand, the first attempts at rational treatment of forecasting were made already when the scientists of the day developed theories in astronomy, movement of objects and heavenly spheres (Ptolemy, Aristotle, Copernicus, Galileo, Newton, Einstein), as well as many other phenomena conditioning advancement of our civilization (sunrises and sunsets, movement of objects in space, sea tides, Earth satellite trajectories, etc.). Therefore, from the onset of time, civilizations have grown accompanied by the functions dedicated to creating and verifying forecasts necessary for important decisions (including business decisions), and to setting up reliable action plans upon those forecasts.

Reliable formal methods of economic forecasting (today we would rather refer to it as business forecasting) did not really exist before the 1930s. It was not until the 1940s and 1950s that scientific formal methods were created. A major progress in this area was noted in particular when those methods were implemented across increasingly popular computers.

Moreover, the 1950s saw a change in the market structure (new global mass products being developed and marketed) that almost forced growth in the sales forecasting methodology.

Further development of forecasting in business was noted at the turn of the 1980s when the information society was being formed. This is when the first functions and departments dedicated to estimation of demand and sales were created. Among the pioneering industries were those related to postal services, consulting, gas and electricity distribution and telecom services. At that time, forecasting was performed at the level of strategic management, when it was necessary to lend reliability to the drawn up strategic plans. This function was set up within the financial and management consulting departments, with forecasts being developed usually by those responsible for the financial performance of a given enterprise.

Over time, sales forecasting has been applied across other industries as well but its growth has been slowest in such areas as manufacturing of consumer goods, new technologies/IT, retail sales, industrial production, services and entertainment (late 1990s). Implementation of sales forecasting was linked to growing market competition and liberalization of access to market information (development of market trend forecasts).

At the same time, individual business areas started to be evaluated according to key performance indicators and were regularly forced to stretch their efficiency limits. As a result, the forecasting function – as one of the key functions – started to be developed independently within such departments as production (operations), purchasing, sales, marketing, market research. This is when the sales prediction was dealt with by market experts, motivated by obtaining the best results by the department they represented. An advantage of such approach was that forecasts were prepared based on a thorough analysis of the market and they took into account multiple aspects and trends.

It should also be taken into account that despite development of many modern forecasting techniques and methods, until recently businesses put into practice forecasting methodologies that dated back to the turn of the 1960s.

Experienced employees of large organizations are well aware that when the forecasting function is dispersed among multiple departments, each with their own KPI reflecting the department's efficiency in a given area, the generated forecasts are often used as tools to support higher efficiency or potential business benefits. This happens especially when those indices are directly related to staff incentive schemes offered by individual departments.

This is illustrated by the following examples.

Sales departments usually receive bonuses for performance which matches or exceeds the plan (measured on either a quantitative or a qualitative basis). Therefore, if such plan is prepared based on a slightly underestimated forecast, it is easier for the entire sales department to perform as planned or even better. Also, the general sales forecast has often reflected the actual market trends, and when dispersed across individual sales areas (markets, regions, channels, customers) it does not necessarily reflect such trends in those areas and the reasons for such inconsistent forecasts and subsequently plans remain inexplicable.

In case of marketing departments that usually receive bonuses for market shares and their growth, generally related to volume and/or value of sales of individual product groups, they are mostly interested in increase of the marketing budgets, so that it is easier for them to achieve respectively higher sales values as a result of 'slightly overestimated' sales projections.

On the one hand, the aforementioned practices are financially detrimental to the organization and on the other, they also cause an organizational inconvenience as there are several forecasts (e.g. financial, sales, marketing, etc.) operating simultaneously within one organization, which creates numerous misunderstandings when the operating departments (production, logistics, purchasing) due to lack of streamlined procedures, are not always certain which forecast to rely on or – what's worse – can select a forecast according to their department's interest, i.e. to achieve the KPI set for their department, such as availability of materials, raw materials or semi-finished products in case of purchasing departments, or availability of finished products in case of production departments.

How those practices and phenomena affect the condition of the entire organization has been discussed in chapter *Importance of Forecasting in Business* (page 14).

Forecasting difficulty – where is the problem?

'Prediction is very difficult, ... especially with regard to the future' said Nils Bohr, the Nobel prize winner, quoting the ironic words purported to be a Chinese proverb. However, there are certain phenomena that are easier to predict than others. What makes a given phenomenon easier or harder to predict? In order to answer this question we should take a closer look at several phenomena subject to forecasting.

Figure 2 - Sun storms and their impact on Earth, source:
https://en.wikipedia.org/wiki/Solar_flare#/media/File:Magnificent_CME_Erupts_on_the_Sun_-_August_31.jpg

Sun Activity, reflected among others by sun storms, is a continual subject of observation and prediction. Sun spots that occur on the Sun lead to the so called solar winds which in consequence are responsible for a myriad of phenomena, such as northern lights, including the disadvantageous ones, i.e. problems with the telecom and electrical networks.

Cyclical nature and increase in this phenomenon are illustrated hereunder:

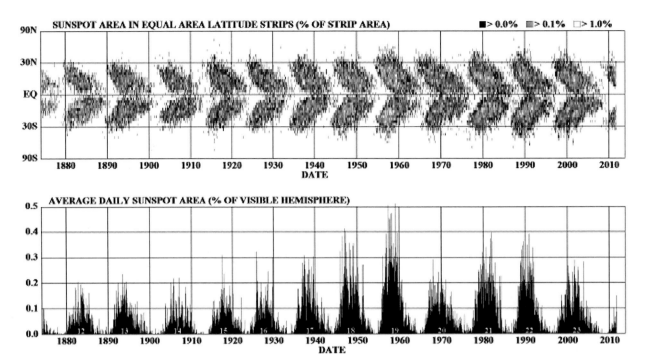

Figure 3 - Average daily sunspot areas for subsequent Earth revolutions around the Sun, source: https://upload.wikimedia.org/wikipedia/commons/9/9e/Sunspot_butterfly_graph.gif?uselang=pl, http://solarscience.msfc.nasa.gov

Another example of this phenomenon, showing the intensity of solar radiation caused by sunspots, is illustrated below:

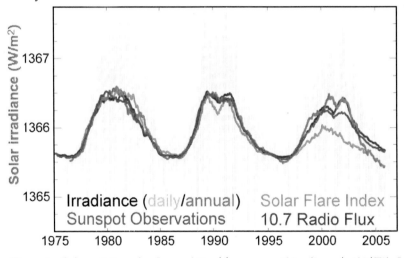

Figure 4 - Solar activity cycles, Source: https://commons.wikimedia.org/wiki/File:Solar-cycle-data.png

Another phenomenon subject to prediction, of a slightly different nature and presenting a different level of forecasting difficulty, is temperature variation on Earth.

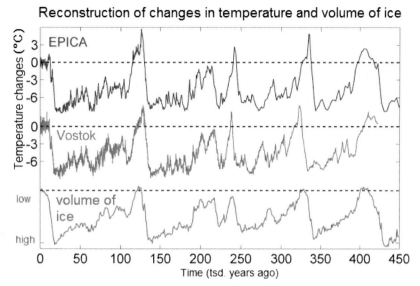

Reconstruction of changes in temperature and volume of ice

Figure 5 - Reconstruction of variation in temperature and ice volume, source:
https://commons.wikimedia.org/wiki/File:Ice_Age_Temperature.png

Another figure shows forecasts of anomalies in global temperatures up to the year 2100:

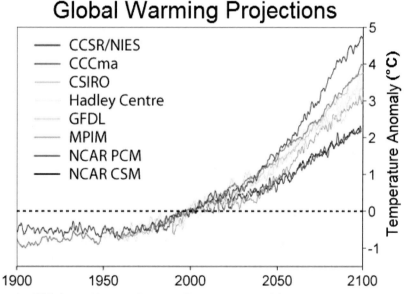

Figure 6 - Global warming projections according to various models, source:
https://commons.wikimedia.org/wiki/File:Global_Warming_Predictions.png

Other phenomena subject to forecasting that in this instance are more directly related to business are prices of ores e.g. silver and gold. The following charts, showing historic prices of such ores, make one wonder about the factors that determine those prices and their forecasts:

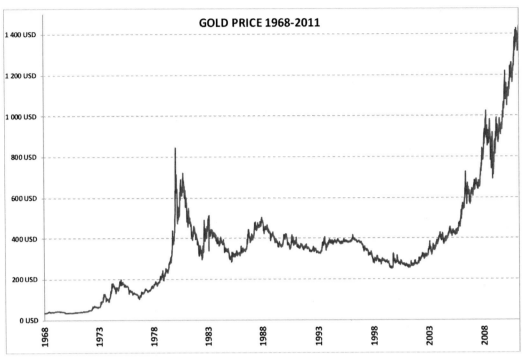

Figure 7 - Prices of gold over the last 40 years, source: The London Bullion Market Association, http://www.lbma.org.uk/precious-metal-prices

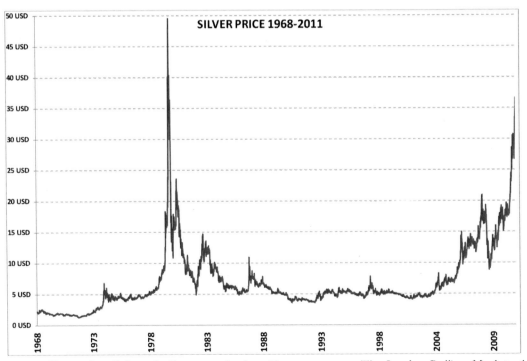

Figure 8 - Prices of silver over the last 40 years, source: The London Bullion Market Association, http://www.lbma.org.uk/precious-metal-prices

An everyday life reference is provided by   the charts showing consumption of alcohol by category:

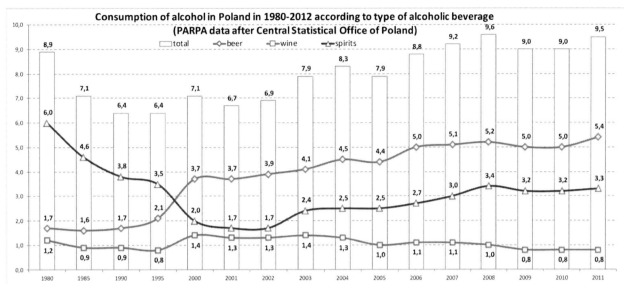

Figure 9 - Alcohol consumption in EU country in 2008-2012 by type of alcoholic beverage. It shows that over the last two decades, the structure of alcohol consumption changed significantly, source: PARPA following GUS

Anyone who studies these charts is likely make certain observations which could serve as a basis for predicting future trends or even values. It must be noted that the described phenomena are set within a certain wider or narrower context. From the point of view of forecasting difficulty, human context is the most difficult one. It means that when human involvement is higher (both in terms of quantity and quality), forecasting a certain phenomenon becomes a bigger challenge. A table presented further on summarizes complexity of the phenomena mentioned earlier, this time taking into account the human factor.

In case of sunspots, people have no impact on what causes them, they are only passive recipients of the consequences. In case of global warming, however, physical factors causing it are changing rather slowly over time but the impact of human factor is high both in terms of quantity (a result of actions of majority of the human population all over the globe) and quality (an effect of a

wide range of human activities in many areas of economy and industry). Changes in gold prices on the other hand are driven by the fact that first of all almost the entire human population perceives gold as a guarantee of value, secondly it is one of those minerals that enabled development of technology and thirdly, for reasons referred to above, it has become a capital investment for many investors, that similarly to money allows to generate added values. Thus, this mineral and its value have become an element of the global economic system. In case of the sales volumes of alcoholic beverages on a given market, fluctuations result not only from changes in individual preferences of consumers but they are also linked to taxation effective on that market and long-term marketing strategies of producers of those beverages.

Considering the above, a conclusion can be drawn with even more certainty that forecasting becomes more difficult and complex as the human factor involved in initiation of a given phenomenon increases and as people become more interested in its effects.

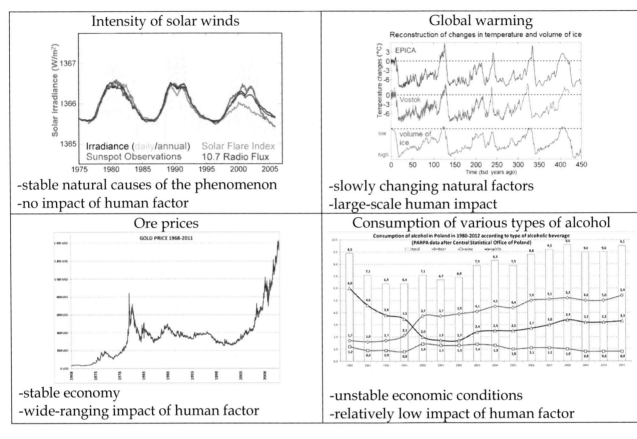

Intensity of solar winds	Global warming
-stable natural causes of the phenomenon -no impact of human factor	-slowly changing natural factors -large-scale human impact
Ore prices	Consumption of various types of alcohol
-stable economy -wide-ranging impact of human factor	-unstable economic conditions -relatively low impact of human factor

Now it is hopefully becoming clear why this book does not tackle the subject of the capital market projections. The reason is rather simple – capital markets are hugely impacted by an unstable human factor. Forecasting in this area does not only require highly developed analytical and organizational skills but also a thorough knowledge of crowd psychology. Considering the aim of this publication, which is introduction to forecasting in a business organization, the aspect of the capital market projections has been intentionally omitted.

Importance of Forecasting in Business

It is not by coincidence that the initial paragraphs of this publication already stress the importance of forecasting in business as in the following chapters the readers will recognize many advantages of high quality forecasts.

Let us assume (hypothetically) that the sales forecasting process is implemented across the organization, its results are measured and it even turns out, over time, that the generated forecasts become ever more precise. This poses a question: how is this important to the organization and the people responsible for implementation and functioning of this process? Such questions become especially important when asked by managers of the organization or its owners who either have invested in this process or intend to and they expect a return on their investment. Nobody with any self-preservation instinct can leave such questions unanswered.

Although at first the answer may seem obvious and banal it is worth pausing for a moment to review the actual and potential results of improving quality of forecasts.

When the list of benefits of the process approach of forecasting is prepared, it is important to communicate it individually and across the organization even if only to increase the awareness and get people to calculate the savings resulting from the process approach to the sales forecasting.

We can go further and try to answer the question how much can our company gain if it takes efforts in order to improve forecasting quality and, in consequence, are those efforts at all worth taking? Generally, there are two areas of benefits that arise from improvement of the sales forecasting quality:

1. **SAVINGS** which are generated mostly in the operational areas of the organization (supply chain, logistics, production)
2. **SALES GROWTH** (volume or value) stemming mostly from elimination of the *'potentially lost sales'*

The impact of the sales forecasts on costs in the operational area is illustrated further on by the analysis which shows how the forecasting influences ROA.

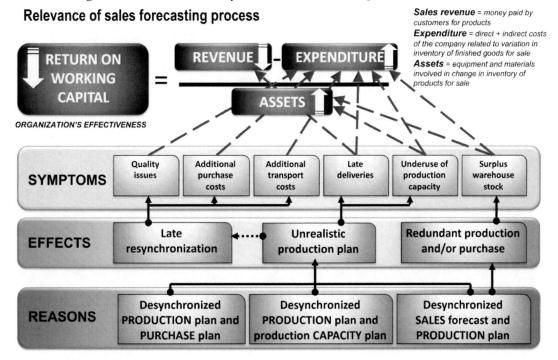

Figure 10 - Forecasting and planning impact on Working Capital shows only one side of the problem – the diagram doesn't include the company's losses from lost sales caused by underestimated market demand and production which fails to meet that demand

It is visible at first glance that lack of synchronization between the demand forecast and the production plan, and consequently the purchase plan (supplies, raw materials, semi-finished goods), negatively impacts the company's financial performance as it generates redundant production – when the sales forecast is overestimated.

When considering what causes such situation it is important to understand that if the sales forecast may change on a day-to-day basis or even as a matter of hours, in case of production plans (especially when there are varied product groups and any change of production plans forces frequent changeovers of production line), and especially purchase plans, such changes are usually not cost free.

Hence, it is so important in business to synchronize all the operational plans with the demand plans but in fact with the sales forecasts (a difference between the two terms is explained in the next chapter) within the appropriately set timeframes (usually a period of 1-3 months, referred to as frozen planning horizons).

The final symptoms which directly impact profit, expenditure and working capital of the company do not require any additional comment. Even if in the situation illustrated above the company management realizes that the sales forecasts are not convergent with the production plans it is usually too late at that stage to introduce any changes to the operational plans.

During one of the conferences dedicated to sales forecasting and operational planning, the results were shown for studies conducted in a large group of companies where the forecasting process was implemented. At those companies, the impact of forecast improvement on the WC was studied and the following formula was delivered as a result:

> **1% SALES FORECASTING IMPROVEMENT MEANS 4% DECREASE IN THE WORKING CAPITAL PER ANNUM!**

Let us look at some realistic market figures for a better insight.

If the organization generates an annual turnover of ca. $150M with the working capital of $30M, if the average aggregated forecast error is 45% its reduction to 35% will bring the working capital down from $30M to ca. $20M and the company will pocket the savings of $10M! These are substantial savings that may be dedicated for instance to business development.

At this point, we may already summarize the general benefits obtained by organizations which implement the forecasting process, stemming not only from savings in the operational areas but also from the advantages recorded in the sales areas:

BENEFITS OF IMPROVED FORECASTS

REDUCTION OF OPERATING EXPENDITUTE

- Reduction of Inventory
- Reduction of Warehouse Space and Transport
- Increase of Productivity of Personnel and Resources
- Reduction of Maintenance Costs
- Reduction of Stock Management Costs

SALES GROWTH

- Improvement of Customer Service
- Reduction of Lost Sales
- Increase of Motivation of the Sales Force
- Reduction of Sales Costs
- Increase of Demand by Improvement of Product Quality
- Reinforcement of Image

Figure 11 - Areas of benefits obtained by improvement of the sales forecasts

When it comes to savings generated by reduction of inventory levels, they refer to the finished goods, as well as raw materials, supplies, semi-finished goods, components, and are realized by direct unfreeze of cash that the company unnecessarily spent on production means or manufactured goods that remained unsold for many months.

Getting rid of this burden allows to handle the logistics needs of the company with the use of smaller warehousing space and reduced number of transport carriers.

In consequence, the employees of production and logistics department are involved in generating fast selling goods, and the production lines are used for appropriately extended and optimized product ranges, while minimizing the changeover and downtime.

As a result of extended production lots,

planned in appropriate advance (without chaotic production line changeovers) and stable sourcing, the manufactured and supplied products show much higher quality, which significantly reduces future service costs on the one hand, and continually strengthens the product, brand and producer image, thus building consumer trust and demand.

It is also important to remember that implementation of the forecasting process is related to ongoing optimization of the product portfolio, namely – in layman's terms – review of the portfolio and tail cutting. Thanks to such regularly undertaken measures, the outlays on administration (both in terms of involvement of human and systemic resources) are substantially reduced. With a well implemented forecasting process, it is also possible to quickly spot the problem areas related to sales and profitability of individual product groups.

And when we think about the benefits of implementing the forecasting processes, gained in the sales areas, we realize that when we manufacture and supply our customers with products which they require at a given time, in the required volumes, we don't risk sending them to our competition for substitutes of products which we are short on. Most often, such customer service quality is expressed by the generally used service level ratio. Sometimes the customer agrees to collect the unavailable goods at a later date, when they become available again. However, in the highly competitive market such customer behavior is rare and may involve products subject to regular offer.

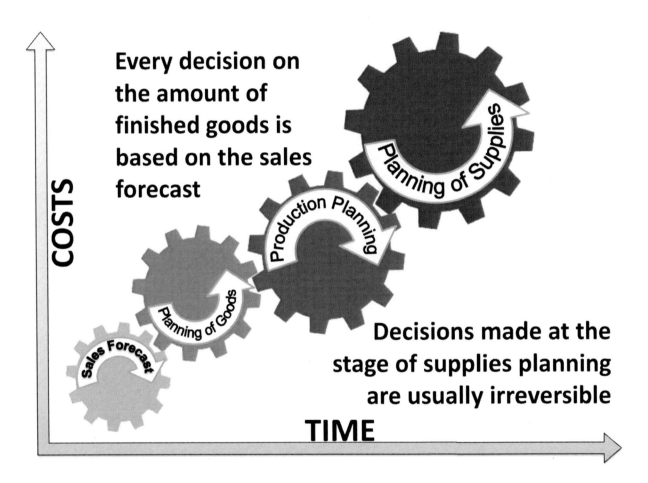

Every decision on the amount of finished goods is based on the sales forecast

COSTS

Planning of Supplies

Production Planning

Planning of Goods

Sales Forecast

Decisions made at the stage of supplies planning are usually irreversible

TIME

Figure 12 - Sales forecasting impact on the Working Capital

Matters are different in case of special offers. Promotions are by definition driven by the sales activities which are preplanned and arranged in due advance, they must have a set start and end date. They are defined by their duration time and usually link into other marketing activities organized by the client (e.g. newsletters) or the producer (e.g. advertising in media) to enjoy the benefits of the economies of scale and synergy. In case of delay in supply of promotional goods to the customer each day of delay causes the irrevocably lost sales and unnecessarily generated costs of advertising enticing customers to purchase the goods which are in fact unavailable.

We should be aware that during that time the consumers will not be interested in the product not included in the promotional offer as the media inform them about the promotion. During the time of promotional sales we observe a cannibalism phenomenon, meaning that the consumer will be interested in the promotional product and if it is unavailable he/she will not buy it at all or will go to our competitor. It is important to understand it not to stress this unfavorable sale phenomenon but to become sensitive to importance of precise forecasting in case of sales promotion.

It is hard to resist the temptation of sharing a certain story here. The described events took place during implementation of the forecasting process at a large company producing and supplying consumer goods to the European market. The company covers a substantial proportion of its portfolio using its own manufacturing resources but it also outsources some production to Asian factories. The sales force decided to run a promotion whereby the locally manufactured products were to be supported by products supplied by the Asian partner. It was a very good and well thought through promotional concept. The sales department ordered the promotional goods in due advance and the ATL actions and the promotional campaign were contracted in the respective sales channels. When the expected promotion time started the products outsourced overseas were indeed overseas or in fact at sea (where they remained for several weeks) and the unfortunate sales team found themselves in a tight spot with no idea how to explain to customers that promotional items are not

and will not be available in any near future. As a consequence, the promotion was cancelled and the regularly offered products were not sold either. In other words, a huge loss was incurred by the company due to:

- lost promotional sales,
- lost regular sales (which would most probably be generated had the consumers not expected the attractive promotion),
- costs of promotion in media and promotion related support offered to agents,

not to mention the strained relationships with the agents that were to run the promotion. A month later, during a standard operating meeting of the sales department, the head of the division where this promotion was to be executed notified the sales team that the almost 'forgotten problem' had just arrived and next month they would have to handle its sales...

This story is not something to be proud of but nevertheless it is educating and true. We need not dwell in detail on why the described events took such course, however, one of the main reasons was – to put it mildly – poor internal communication which is one of key elements of implementation of the forecasting process.

It goes without saying that when the sales people found out that apart from the scheduled sales they would need to quickly deal with the sales of problematic products, the level of their motivation to undertake sales efforts significantly dropped and, as a result, execution of the entire plan also suffered. It is vital to understand that this type of behaviour (reaction) of the sales staff when faced with such challenges is a rule rather than an exception and it stems from lack of process approach to forecasting. It is also clear that the company had to pay hefty fines for failure to deliver the promotional goods to the agents. A healthy forecasting system in place can at the very least help avoid such unnecessary costs.

Situations similar to the one referred to above put a strain on cooperation and are often used by the clients when negotiating annual contracts and/or commercial terms. We are all well aware that in today's world business is built on long-term relationships and trust, therefore any growth oriented company cannot afford such incidents.

For the same reason why maintenance costs are reduced in the operational area, product, brand and producer image are reinforced in the commercial areas, which in consequence stimulates consumer demand and, naturally, the sales increase.

It is worth stressing once again that focusing sales efforts on one-off sales (without clearance sales of non-rotating products or unsold promotional merchandise) significantly increases motivation and productivity of the valuable human resources.

These arguments and the described events (which could take place at many companies), should encourage readers to reflect on whether forecasting is a process which aids their business or it requires appropriate measures and actions to be taken in order to become such aid.

To wrap up the arguments for importance of forecasting in business, please find below one approach to quantification of costs stemming from low quality of the sales forecasts. This approach is expressed by the following formula:

$$COI = \frac{\sum(Cost_{OverFct} + Cost_{UnderFct})}{\frac{\sum(MAPE)}{n}} * 100$$

where:

COI – *cost of inaccuracy (forecast inaccuracy of 1%/1pp),*

Cost_{OverFct} – *estimated cost of forecast overestimation,*

Cost_{UnderFct} – *estimated cost of forecast underestimation,*

MAPE – *forecast inaccuracy expressed by mean absolute percentage error; this error is described further on in the chapter on measurement of forecast quality,*

n – *nominal number of percentage points which the cost will be referring to.*

Let us assume that we set a monthly cost of overestimation in a given product group at a level of $120.000, the cost of underestimation at the level of $82.500, and the calculated MAPE for that product group is 45% and the cost has been calculated nominally for n = 1 pp. It stems from calculations that every 1%/1pp of the forecast error costs $4.500, and thus, an improvement of forecast accuracy by 15%/15pp may result in the monthly savings of $65.000.

Although such calculation is a simplification, it may prove to be a useful instrument for estimating the costs incurred and, what's more, for calculating a return on investment in implementation of the forecasting process across the organization.

The next chapter aims to systematize certain terms related to forecasting and embedding of the forecasting process in an organization. It also offers a general review of the forecasting methods and defines the basic rules of forecasting.

SUMMARY

- forecasting as a discipline is well known and has been used for centuries, however, thanks to advancement in technology and wide access to information in the recent years, its importance in business organizations is increasing and it is often introduced in coordination of the sales processes, marketing and management of supply chain,
- challenges in the forecasting area are increasing proportionally to impact of the human factor and complexity of the economic area subject to forecasting,
- importance of forecasting in business stems from advantages it delivers in two areas:
  - o operational savings,
  - o increase in the level of sales and reduction of the sales costs,
- profits from implementation of the forecasting process may range from a few percent to a few dozen percent of the company's turnover and may be measured if the organization has an advanced controlling system in place.

2. Basics

In this chapter...
- Basic terms related to forecasting and correlations between them,
- Review and streamlining of information on forecasting methods, their types and limitations,
- Fundamental forecasting laws.

Basic Terms and Definitions

First let us define the meaning of forecasting. When browsing through literature and other available resources (Internet), we encounter numerous definitions which are more or less alike. Nevertheless, for the purposes of further reading, let us assume a general and quite simple definition:

> **FORECASTING** means to form statements regarding a certain state or event that will occur in the future.
>
> The following can be subject to forecasting:
> - **events** - their nature and when they occur,
> - **changes** - trends, changes in trends and their structures,
> - **probability** - risk or certainty that certain events or states will occur in the future.

In the business context it is worth to perform a brief review of those elements of business that must definitely be subject to forecast. The major ones are shown in Figure 13 but of key importance for our purposes are those that are related to sales.

> **DEMAND FORECAST** is a view regarding the level of purchasing capacity of the market (consumers, customers) at a specific time in the future, in specific market conditions.
>
> **SALES FORECAST** is a view regarding the level of sales at a specific time in the future, in specific market conditions.

Therefore, for this business area we should specify what demand forecast is and what sales forecast is and why these are not always the same terms.

Why these terms are not always the same and should be set apart? Well, the production or logistic resources are limited and oftentimes they are insufficient to satiate the demand on a given market. In such situations the **demand forecast** (most often expressed as a summary order declared by customers) is knowingly verified down to the level of operational capacity of the organization (production / logistics capacity), thus becoming a realistic **sales forecast**. Such situations often take place when we deal with a newly introduced product or product category in the first and second stage of life, when it becomes a market hit and the production capacity is insufficient to meet the growing demand.

Can it happen that the sales forecast is higher than the demand forecast? If we differentiate between the agent demand (agent understood as market participant, i.e. sales channel, wholesalers, distribution networks or retailers) and the customer demand (final recipient and consumer of given goods or services), the sales mechanisms of the producer may occur and generate a higher sales demand on among market agents than the actual customer demand recorded at the same time. This occurs e.g. when seasonal products are prepared for sales and it is aimed at stocking the distribution channels so that the product is available to the customer via all the channels earmarked for distribution when the season begins (this stems from 'inertia' of distribution on a wide scale and/or limitation of production capacity). Similar situations take place when new products are introduced to the market. Usually such market launch is supported by a strong promotional and media campaign and the producer aims for the product to be shelf ready for the customers as soon as such campaign starts. In such case also the sales mechanisms are launched, causing the sales forecast to exceed the demand forecast.

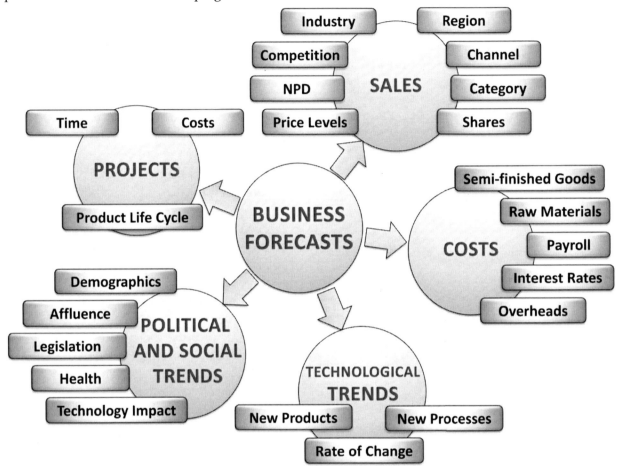

Figure 13 - Key business forecasting areas

While continuing to review the basic terms, we should also be aware of what forecasting means in the context of all kinds of plans and planning. It is a very important aspect as forecasting and planning are activities with completely different objectives, while many managers treat these terms interchangeably. The meaning of forecast and plan is different even though these terms are definitely connected.

In majority of companies, the sales plan comes with the closely related **sales support plans** (e.g. marketing, promotion, media plans, etc.). A particular type of sales plan is the **annual sales plan** which is also referred to as the target, budget, etc. It is usually prepared by the company management and it forms one of the key elements of the strategic plan.

In practice, the annual plan, as a strategy

element, is prepared first (usually at the end of the sales year which is not always the same as the calendar year), and by dividing it into individual periods and market segments (while taking into consideration actual information and trends), **detailed sales plans** are being developed.

Only on the basis of the sales plans (the annual sales plan and the periodic plans within) the **operational planning** is performed, i.e.:

- purchase of raw materials, semi-finished goods and components is planned,
- production is planned (scheduling production, planning change-overs, maintenance and repairs of production lines, etc.),
- investments are planned (e.g. purchase / lease of production lines or outsourcing of production),
- employment is planned (e.g. FTEs and seasonal employees).

At this point, it is worth to ask what is the relationship between forecasting and all those plans?

The **annual sales plan** results from the following:

1. sales plan, strongly supported by the prevailing market trends and the identified effects of seasonality of specific products,
2. strategic plan of the company and plans of activities supporting that plan (e.g. introduction of new products, promotion plans, etc.).

Credibility of the **sales plans** for individual periods (months, quarters) and market segments (channels, regions, agents) is provided cyclically by the sales forecasts generated for the specific periods and market segments. The forecasts are a measure of credibility and feasibility of the earlier plans, and if such credibility is questioned, the appropriate changes may be forced upon the management, i.e.:

1. change of the sales plans for specific periods,
2. change of the sales plans in individual market segments,
3. change of the action plans supporting sales, most often boiling down to reallocation of the supporting resources (most often known as marketing, promotional budgets, etc.) as the strategic plan usually allocates a predefined fixed budget for support, that remains an unchanging Total for the whole year.
4. changes in all the aforesaid areas and aspects simultaneously, and business practice shows that such action is the most common.

It stems from the above that the forecasting process is superior to the planning processes and controls them.

A meaningful reference that presents the relationship between forecasting and planning is the story of the yacht cruise which by way of analogy to the discussed terms and processes speaks directly to imagination.

Let us assume that the objective is to travel by yacht from port A to port B in a period of 6 months. With the knowledge of atmospheric conditions from previous years, in periods corresponding to the time of our trip, we may project with high probability which winds (strength and directions) we may expect throughout our entire journey:

- Month 1: Southwest wind 6
- Month 2: West wind 7
- Months 3-4: North wind 8
- Months 5-6: Northwest wind 3

We also know that in a straight line between the ports there is an archipelago of dangerous islands and underwater rocks which must be bypassed in a wide angle. The plan of this cruise is illustrated hereunder:

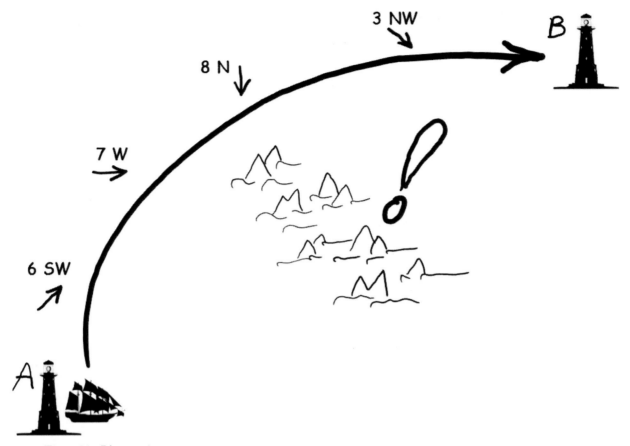

Figure 14 - Plan - cruise map

The departing yacht may have enough food for 7 months of cruising and enough petrol to run on engine in case of emergency – without the use of sails - for 7 days.

With this information at hand, future weather conditions and projected and thereupon, as well as on the basis of the available resources, an optimum cruise route is planned, i.e. the quickest and cheapest in terms of the available resources. The captain and the team and experienced sailors so they primarily use the wind.

After sailing out, during the cruise, the team is continually receiving information about the existing and forecast weather conditions. When approaching a chain of islands, the team obtains the weather forecast according to which this year the winds will change their direction in this region 3 weeks earlier than usually (as planned at the beginning of the cruise). In view of this information the captain must make a decision to bypass the dangerous islands from the opposite direction than previously planned, which will cause approximately a 7-day delay. It would of course be possible to stay on the original cruise plan, however – for safety reasons – using just the engine for around 6 days would run a real risk that if petrol runs out the yacht may get smashed against the rocks of one of the islands or it may hit shallow waters.

Figure 15 - Adjusted cruise plan

The captain, however, decides that the yacht will not cruise against the wind and instead it will bypass the chain of islands from the opposite side even though this maneuver will add around 7 days to the total cruise time. On the other hand, the weather anomaly consisting in an earlier change of the wind direction will allow the team to bypass the islands and underwater rocks from the opposite direction than previously planned, which may accelerate the cruise by around 3-4 days, and at its final phase the sails may be used together with the engine (even though more orthodox sailors will not feel comfortable with this), which will allow to gain speed, make up for the lost time and arrive at the destination port as projected or even slightly earlier.

This story shows how important it is to gain information on where we are at a certain time, generate and obtain forecasts, analyze them and make decisions that are safe on the one hand and optimal on the other hand from the point of view of the assumed mission purpose.

By analogy to the described cruise, it clearly shows that the **forecasting function** is a kind of navigator on a sailing yacht, responsible for the following:

1. **reliable information** about where we are at a given time
2. **forecasting** where we will end up if the present conditions prevail, and
3. **recommendations for the captain** as to review of the cruise plan in order to complete it as planned.

The symbolic meaning of this brief sailing story which may refer to every business reality is quintessential to the forecasting function and it shows it in context of any

kind of planning.

Review of Forecasting Methods

This section is aimed at explaining to the 'outsiders' and reminding the 'insiders' the general forecasting methodology. The diagram (Figure 16 below) shows the general topology[1] and the basic methods used in the sales forecasting processes.

As you can see, forecasting methods may be generally divided into:

- **Objective**, in other words statistical or other methods based on formal analytical methods,
- **Subjective**, namely the methods of inference based principally on people's views and judgments.
- and the so called **'Prophesies'**, i.e. a special group of views regarding the past, that are based on neither the rational premises nor any express methods of inference; they are often an inexpressive form of guessing or an expression of ambitions and personal goals of top managers. Although from the methodological point of view this type of forecasting is not rationally justified, communicating such *forecasts* by those managers often causes for many of them to become at last partially *self-fulfilling prophesies* that truly, even if contrarily, influence future reality. And although from the methodical point of view the analytical purists may not accept such practices, from the business point of view such practices, as a knowingly used tool, are valuable as they force certain actions

which will change future reality.

However, let us return to our discussion of objective and subjective methods. In the area of **objective methods** we identify methods based on **analysis of time series** and methods based on **analysis of cause and effect** relationships between various phenomena.

In case of methods based on analysis of **time series**, it is assumed that occurrence of a certain phenomenon in the future (its value, scale, quality, etc.) is closely related to its past performance.

Thus, the mathematical models 'observing' a certain phenomenon in the past can predict its behaviour in the future.

Time series methods are unrivalled when it comes to ease of implementation across all types of computer systems supporting forecasting. This is due to accessibility of models and moderate requirements regarding the amount of gathered data on the history of the observed phenomenon (e.g. sales).

Those are the methods that are accessed first of all – which is fully justified as when making a decision on the forecasting process support, we obtain quickly a noticeable improvement of forecasts with relatively low outlays. Therefore, this book pays more attention to those methods, presenting in a greater detail their premises, general approach and classification.

---

[1] You may find much more complex topologies in other studies

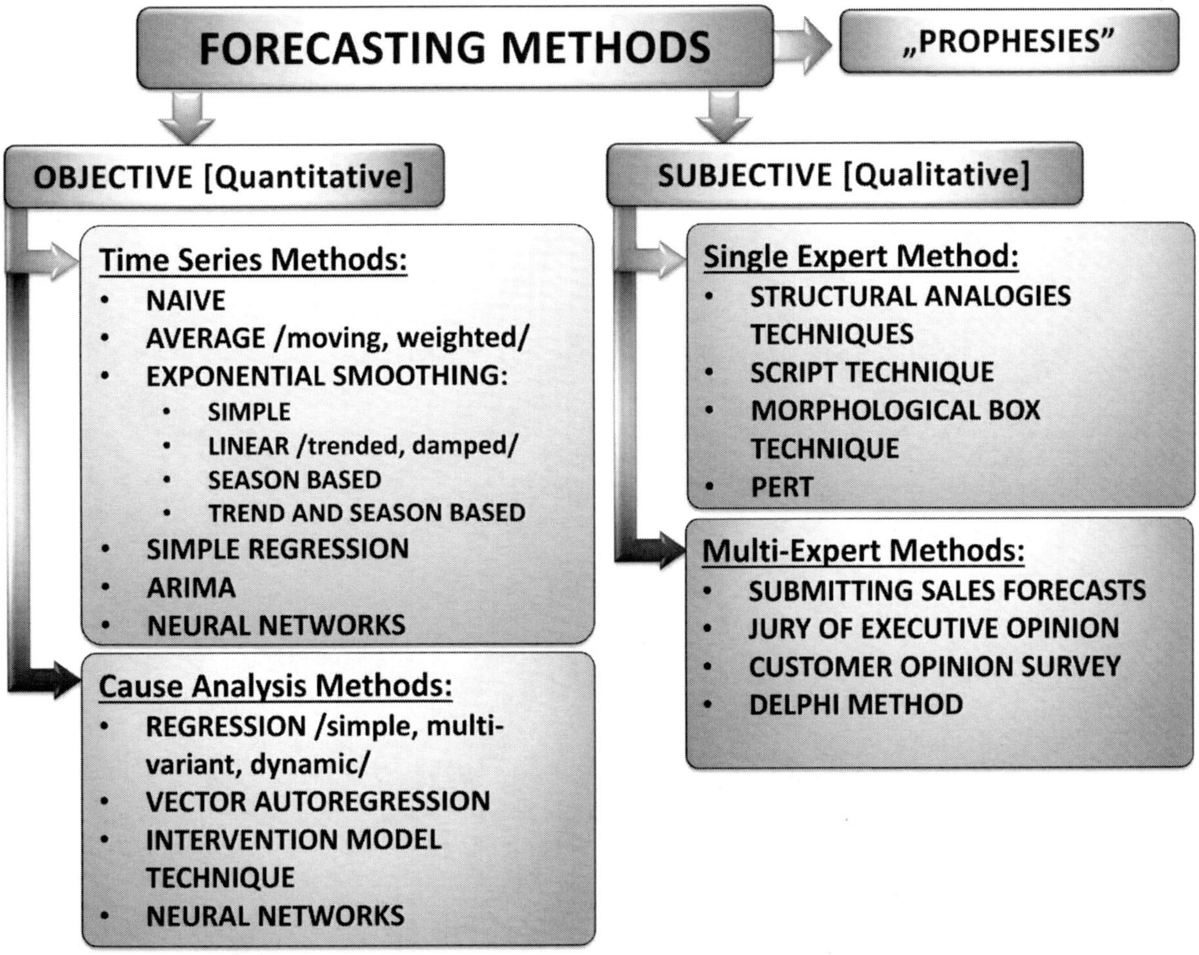

FORECASTING METHODS → „PROPHESIES"

OBJECTIVE [Quantitative]

Time Series Methods:
- NAIVE
- AVERAGE /moving, weighted/
- EXPONENTIAL SMOOTHING:
  - SIMPLE
  - LINEAR /trended, damped/
  - SEASON BASED
  - TREND AND SEASON BASED
- SIMPLE REGRESSION
- ARIMA
- NEURAL NETWORKS

Cause Analysis Methods:
- REGRESSION /simple, multi-variant, dynamic/
- VECTOR AUTOREGRESSION
- INTERVENTION MODEL TECHNIQUE
- NEURAL NETWORKS

SUBJECTIVE [Qualitative]

Single Expert Method:
- STRUCTURAL ANALOGIES TECHNIQUES
- SCRIPT TECHNIQUE
- MORPHOLOGICAL BOX TECHNIQUE
- PERT

Multi-Expert Methods:
- SUBMITTING SALES FORECASTS
- JURY OF EXECUTIVE OPINION
- CUSTOMER OPINION SURVEY
- DELPHI METHOD

Figure 16 - General forecasting methods

General premises of the time series methodology:
- the obtained measurements of the phenomenon include:
  - REGULAR PART (scheduled) and
  - RANDOM PART (unscheduled),
- but unfortunately we are not able to observe and measure these components separately,
- applied forecasting methods try to isolate the systematic part from the random part,
- forecasting methods are mostly based on the systematic part,
- the data, describing the phenomenon over time, is comparative, i.e.:
  - time of measurement is the same,
  - measurement units do not change over time,
  - definition (terminology) of the measured object remains unchanged,
  - measurements are performed correctly,
- errors in measurements of data occur as a result of the sampling process, as there are mistakes in the measuring tools or as a result of copying data.

The main patterns of time series are presented in Figure 17 below:

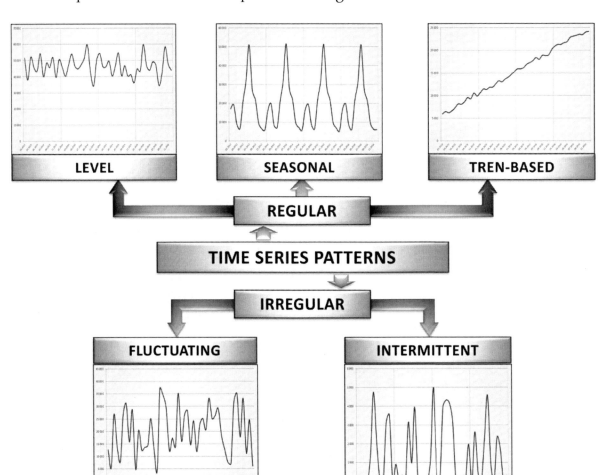

Figure 17 - Basic patterns of time series

The **LEVEL** (horizontal) time series pattern is determined by a certain fixed level of a given phenomenon (e.g. sales) and the random fluctuations. The **SEASONAL** time pattern is a sum total of a certain level of the phenomenon, seasonality and random fluctuations. The **TREND** time series pattern is determined by the trend factor added to the initial level of the phenomenon and the random fluctuations. The irregular **FLUCTUATING** time series is one that is characterized by very strong fluctuations around a specific level the phenomenon, where an average standard deviation from values is higher than half of the medium value from all the observations. And the time series referred to as **INTERMITTENT** (or sporadic) is one where the number of periods without recording the phenomenon (sales) is relatively high (30-40%).

It is obvious that such clean patterns are not the only ones that occur in a business reality. Other known time series patterns arise by way of appropriate combination of the basic patterns or combination with irregular phenomena treated more like interruptions and hence not mentioned in the basic definitions. The irregular phenomena (interruptions) include among others:

- **NOISE** – random deformations an interruptions which occur in each phenomenon being observed,

- **PULS, OUTLIER** – sporadic, single variation (increase / decrease) in the observed phenomenon level (e.g. can be caused by a new type of promotional sales) – Figure 18 below,

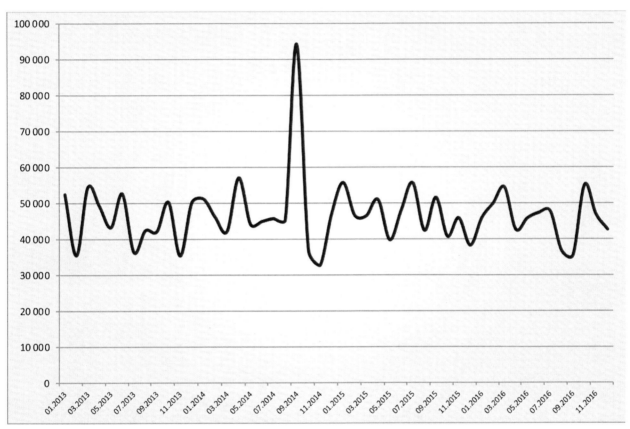

Figure 18 - Interruption - PULS, OUTLIER

- **LEVEL SHIFT, OUTLIER PATCH** – sporadic, one-time or many-time level variation that lasts for several periods (may be caused by a long-term attractive sales offer e.g. due to brand / producer anniversary),
- **STRUCTURAL BREAK** – periodic break in the observed systematic phenomenon (can be caused by e.g. disclosure of qualitative product issues or strong activity of the competition) – Figure 19.

The listed interruptions may occur in combination with all of the basic patterns (fixed, trend, seasonal).

For reasons of convenience the following abbreviations have been adopted for the individual components of the time series patterns and shall be used further on:

- **A** (actual) – obtained or resulting value of the phenomenon (e.g. sales quantity or value),
- **L** (level) – fixed component

- **S** (season) – seasonality component,
- **T** (trend) – trend component,
- **E** (error) – random component (errors, noise).

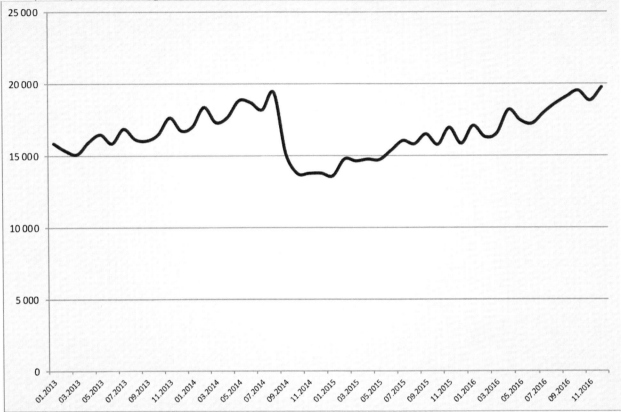

Figure 19 - Interruption - STRUCTURAL BREAK

We adopt two arithmetic operations for combination of patterns: adding and multiplying (modulating). As a result of those operations we arrive at a matrix of patterns shown in Figure 20 below. This list of patterns also offers suggestions of methods that best support forecasting individual combinations of time series patterns.

This list leads to a natural question: how to forecast such complex patterns? Well, the answer is just as natural... it is necessary to separate the individual components, forecast separately and put together again.

Another question arises: How to do this? In all honesty it is no longer a simple task and it requires either 1) great experience in observing and identifying patterns and components of time series, or 2) good system supporting analysis of time series, that can break complex series into basic components and calculate optimal parameters of the basic models within. Today's computer technology – with the available statistical data or the signal theory – allow already to undertake such task and successfully complete it. For basic information, guidelines or advice in this area follow the chapter *Additional materials* (page 168).

As mentioned in the introduction, the reader will not find in this publication detailed descriptions of all the forecasting methods, together with the mathematical formula. Others have done so and here let me refer you to the specialist literature. Nevertheless, for convenience reasons they have been briefly described so that every

reader can understand individual methods and which time series types each of them is applied to and why.

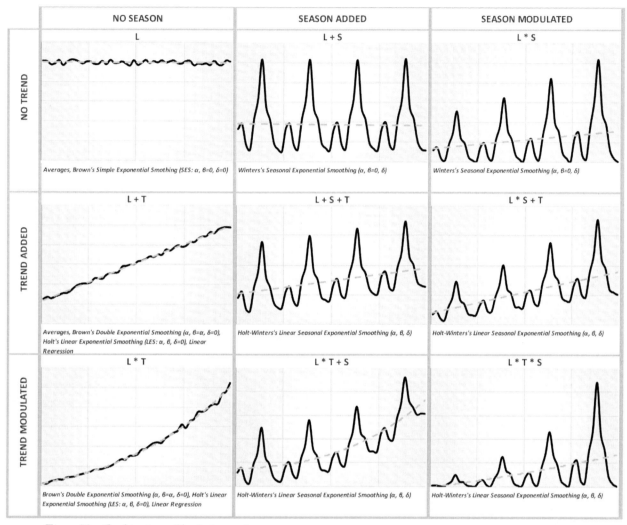

Figure 20 - Combinations of basic time series patterns

The readers who deal in implementation of forecasting models in the IT tools (from spreadsheets through to dedicated forecasting systems) are encouraged to read the chapter 5. Forecasting Methodologies and Models (page 145) which analyses some selected forecasting models for time series – from the most simple to the most advanced ones.

The main statistical methods, specified

earlier in the figure and applied to time series, are as follows:

- **Naive Method** – this method assumes that the forecast value equals the value of the last observation,
- **Average** – this method assumes that the forecast value will equal arithmetic average for all the available observations,
- **Moving Averages** – this method forecasts the value based on an arithmetic average

of the specific number of last observations (e.g. 3-month, 6-month, 12-month/annual moving average, etc.)

- **Brown's Single Exponential Smoothing** – the method based on the exponentially weighted moving average; it is dedicated to time series with fixed characteristics – the forecast is determined only by the sales level (L),
- **Holt's Linear Exponential Smoothing** – the basic assumptions of this method are the same as for SES but it is dedicated to series with trend; therefore, apart from the element of the model responsible for forecasting appropriate level (L), the model includes an additional element responsible for following the changeable, by assumption, trend (T).
- **Gardner's Damped Trend Exponential Smoothing** – the model is an extension on the LES model, including the trend dampening over time; this prevents, among others, forecasting an indefinite increase of the sales level or forecasting negative sales values in a downtrend situation; the trend dampening rate is controlled with an appropriate φ parameter selected for that model,
- **Winters' Seasonal Exponential Smoothing** – similarly to Linear Exponential Smoothing, it is an advancement on the basic method, however, it provides for an element of seasonality in the time series: this is aided by introduction of the element responsible for identification and forecasting of the seasonality factor (S) in the model; the idea of this factor is similar to the basic SES and LES,
- **Holt-Winters' Trend-Seasonal Exponential Smoothing** – as its very name suggests it is a combination of Holt's and Winters' models and incorporates in the forecast all 3 elements,

i.e. level (L), trend (T) and seasonality (S), which are controlled by way of selection of parameters α, β, δ, respectively.

Presented above are all major statistical forecasting methods for the basic time series and their most simple combinations. Formal descriptions of those models have been set out in one of the following chapters related to methodology, which present not only the formulas but also examples of their implementation in the spreadsheet.

Having become acquainted with the major statistical methods, let us briefly discuss the most important ones of the subjective forecasting methods mentioned earlier:

- **The Poll of Sales Force Opinion** – expert method that uses extensive market knowledge from customers (i.e. trends, market fluctuations, changes in channels, consumer purchases that show changes in purchase behaviour). It consists in individually asking members of the sales forces about their estimates of sales by product and further on by channel, region (according to the sales forces structure); useful questions: *What is your estimated sales / of new product / to the customer / in the promotional / marketing campaign in the upcoming month / quarter / year?*; as the next step the collected estimates are aggregated for specific products, regions, etc.; Unfortunately, this method shows weaknesses related to: 1) lack of skills of the sales forces in the area of statistical methods and frequent tendency to estimate using a naive method, 2) insufficient understanding of the weight o submitted information and limited effort in this regard, 3) individual tendency to either over or underestimate. In a nutshell: there are many problems related to this method but it offers a possibility to obtain a lot of valuable information; the method is useful for operational forecasting and planning.

- **The Jury of Executive Opinion** – this method consists in collecting subjective opinions of the mid and top level executives with knowledge of the company's business. It lies in the following: 1) one-to-one meetings, 2) meetings in groups with moderated discussion, 3) drawing conclusions from the held meetings and translating them into forecast. Similarly as in the case of the earlier method, this one also has limitations related to: 1) low statistical methods skills, 2) dissonance between various points of view, 3) group inclinations Despite these limitations, it offers valuable – even if often informal – information, and it is used in tactical forecasting and medium term planning.

- **The Survey of Customer's Buying Plans** – entails obtaining from customers information regarding their future buying plans via individually shaped and structural interviews or using surveys. The main weaknesses of this method include: 1) it is hard to prepare convincing and reliable survey (use the scale of 1-5 or 1-7, appropriately designed questions, length of survey), 2) need to conduct tests before and after the survey, 3) individual inclinations, 4) company policy, 5) undisclosed problems.

- **The Delphi Method** – is a structured expert forecasting process. Its strengths include: 1) possibility to apply to large groups of geographically dispersed experts by taking advantage of office bundles or workflow software; 2) avoiding impact of certain individuals on others by way of preserving anonymous status; on the other hand this method can be time consuming and, therefore, costly,

especially that we are talking about the time of top earning experts. Execution of this method boils down to several stages:

- o an initial stage when experts – participants of the panel - are selected – and sent to them are surveys asking for their opinions regarding the forecast values,
- o panel participants contribute their forecasts independently and anonymously (!),
- o the results of surveys are summed up and feedback is sent, incorporating the following:
  - each individual forecast should be presented in a table together with summary,
  - feedback should additionally include information on averages, medians and scope of the forecasting values (min/max),
  - feedback should be offered while at the same time asking the experts whether they would like to amend their forecasts or provide a comment,
- o this is followed by the next stage when the experts, having received the specifications and statistics, decide to either leave or amend their forecasts,
- o the process is repeated until reaching the level of consensus on the projected values or there are no amendments of individual forecasts by the experts; in case of discrepancies between the final estimates the final forecast is the median from the obtained results.

- **The Projection of Past Sales Method** – this method entails identification of a similar sales phenomenon (introduction of a similar product, similar marketing campaign, similar sales promotion, etc.), as compared to the planned one, and its value is estimated by way of indicating the corresponding elements, such as timeline, area, duration, regional potential, etc. Figure 21 hereunder shows

an example of such specification for estimation:

Promotion Start Date	Promotion Type	Duration	Region	Sales Value
30.IV	'3+1'	3 weeks	Country 1	$270 TSD
5.VI	'3+1'	3 weeks	Country 2	$310 TSD
11.VIII	'3+1'	2 weeks	Country 3	$240 TSD

Figure 21 - Example of Structural Analogies Technique

When using the subjective methods, it is worth taking into account several practical comments that facilitate their use:

- if the forecast is to be generated by a group of experts (specialists, managers), it is best to use the Delphi Method,
- in case the panel of experts is unavailable, it is best to use the Projection of Past Sales Method,
- it is necessary to simplify complex forecasting tasks – i.e. to first forecast on the level of regions or sales channels and then, on that basis, provide a complete forecast,
- statistical forecasts should be verified using expert (subjective) forecasts only when there is vital, additional information about the upcoming events at hand (information that is definitely not included in the statistical forecasts),
- subjective methods should be used in forecasting only when:
  o there is no historical data on the phenomenon or the amount of available data is very limited,
  o the available data is not quantifiable,
  o there is sufficient access to the qualitative knowledge of the relations with the examined phenomenon,
- one should ask for reasons of verification of forecasts by experts and record answers,
- only in justified cases it is worth considering combination of several methods.

Weaknesses of Expert Methods

It is necessary to be aware that expert methods, as they are based on people's opinions, are always encumbered with a certain bias. This stems among others from:

- **Availability of facts and ability to remember them** – considering human factor, probability of a future event is estimated on the basis of how easy it is to remember and bring back a similar past event; in other words, when forming opinions we are influenced by what we remember best → the forecasts are determined by current and spectacular events (media role aside...).

- **Anchoring and adjustments** – when beginning to project, people usually first specify the initial value (the so called *anchor value*) – usually the value that is last remembered, and next they are searching for a final forecast around that anchor value; in this way the final forecast is usually not too remote from the anchor.

- **Extrapolation of noise** – when extrapolating the duration of the time series people expect that future behaviour patterns will resemble the past ones; thus the past patterns get copied into the forecast together with the noise.

- **Group inclinations** – the forecast is formed under the influence of dominant and eloquent individuals and *'evangelic'* forecasts of executives.

To summarize the above: verifications of forecasts based on human heuristics are usually not optimal.

Please find below a brief comparison of objective and subjective methods, to wrap up this chapter:

OBJECTIVE methods	SUBJECTIVE methods
• Formal mathematical models and systematic instructions how to generate forecasts (with formal methods) • Methods used on the same data always result in the same forecast regardless of time or person who generated it • Are NOT based on experience and expertise of the forecasting staff • Are also referred to as QUANTITATIVE methods	• Informal and unspecific human way of thinking without methodical forecast generation instructions • Heuristics based on subjective experience and expert knowledge • Forecasting results are not repetitive in case of various experts or even the same expert at different times • Are also referred to as QUALITATIVE or JUDGEMENTAL methods

Figure 22 - Comparison of objective and subjective methods

For more clearance, let me explain the general **difference** between the objective **time-series** methods and the **casual** methods:

- the time series methods recognize a pattern of past behaviour and assume its continuation in the future,
- the casual models identify dependencies between the phenomena (dependent and independent variables) and while accepting them as true, they draw conclusions about the phenomenon to occur in the future in their context.

The artificial neural network methods may be applied to both types of objective methods due to ability to *'teach'* the network to recognize both the time series patterns and the relationship between the phenomena.

Nevertheless, the business practice of global companies representing many industries shows conclusively that the best results are obtained by way of using the objective (statistical methods) with an adjustment made with subjective methods.

Fundamental Forecasting Rules

At the end of this section let us go over a certain set of rules which help the adepts (and not just the adepts) not to get lost in the daily challenges related to forecasting and organization of this process:

I.   Improvement of forecasts using the *'human factor'* is a must as blind trust in automatic computer forecasts may be dangerous!

II.   It is required to forecast on the SKU and the location.

III. Forecasting on a higher level of aggregation will always be more precise.

IV.   A regular measurement of the forecast error is necessary.

V.   It is important to manage the forecasting process via exceptions (a rule generally known as → the Pareto Principle).

VI.   There is no single method that allows to correctly forecast all the phenomena and their time series (→ the main problem of business forecasting: selection and application of alternative methods is up to the process manager).

VII. There is no reliable, fully automated forecasting detection method in the systems supporting forecasting (e.g. APO, i2), although there are several good ones (→ expert knowledge is required in order to make decisions as to automation of the forecasting support systems).

VIII. NEVER use forecasting methods which you don't fully understand! (it is vital to know the capacity of that method, its weaknesses and problems which may accompany its use).

SUMMARY
- Forecasting is not planning or posing goals although these actions are interrelated.
- Demand forecast does not equal the sales forecast.
- There are objective and subjective forecasting methods – business practice shows that the best results are obtained when both types are used respectively.
- It is most important when using the forecasting methods to fully understand them.
- Regular measurement of the forecast quality is a necessity.

The next chapter discusses an aspect of people to take responsibility for process management and forecasting methodology: their discretion and number, which areas of company operations they represent, what should be their position in the organization's structures and hierarchy and the challenges ahead.

3. Sales Forecasting Team

In this chapter...
- forecasting and SOP process models at organizations,
- who should assume responsibility for the forecasting process and what does it depend on,
- what should be the discretions of the leader and his/her team responsible for the forecasting process,
- how to select the appropriate team number,
- optimal location of the forecasting team within the organizational structure and hierarchy.

Forecasting and SOP Function Models

The Sales Forecasting Process chapter discusses issues related to organization of the forecasting process across the company. However, before diving into those discussions, we need to first determine who at the company should assume responsibility for forecasting.

The first chapter indicates that forecasting function, although it is by no means an old discipline, has already undergone a certain evolution. Originally, as a central function of strategic forecasting, it would be usually placed somewhere within the management board or the financial and controlling divisions. At the next stage of its evolution, as a result of decentralization the function would get dispersed within the R&D, Purchasing, Production, Sales and Marketing divisions, which usually led to several forecasts being forked up at the company. This was certainly not a desired result even if quality of those forecasts was high as they were prepared by staff with a lot of experience and a thorough knowledge of the product and the market.

Having more than one forecast at hand does create a multitude of problems related to executive decisions, hence the reverse trend to centralize this function, and even to develop and prepare it so that it is possible to integrate forecasting processes not just on a level of a single organization but also many organizations that create a chain for supplying products (or services) to the end consumer.

At companies – and organizations in general – 4 stages of development of this function may be noted:

- **Stage 1: Function Focus** – in this form the forecasting and planning processes are run independently, as part of the company's individual functions/divisions (Sales, Marketing, Production, Purchases, R&D, Finance, etc.).

> *Example*: *the Production Department optimizes the production batch size using the system tool; at the same time, independently, the Logistics Department optimizes the warehousing space and the Sales Department forecasts future sales amounts on the basis of analysis of the historical data.*

- **Stage 2: Internal Integration** – at this stage of development of the organization there is an inter-functional integration of forecasting processes and systems and operational planning; the company's effectiveness is substantially increased and the desired business results are more easily attained.

> *Example*: *Implementation of the SCM process which improves communication of the parties involved (commercial and operational departments) while generating one ultimate forecast/plan and simultaneously implementing and integrating the SOP system with the ERP system of the company. As a result the entire company benefits from sustained used of fixed assets and WC, optimization of inventory levels and increase of customer service.*

- **Stage 3: External Integration** – at this stage, the planning and forecasting processes are executed together with the customers or direct suppliers.

Example: Direct communication between the organizational units of cooperating companies (supplier / producer / distributor) as part of joint business undertaking, consisting among others in offering forecasts and online plans for access and verification. Implementation of VMI class and CPFR systems.

- **Stage 4: External Cooperation and Optimization** – actions performed at this stage boil down to joint development of forecasts and plans and optimization of those processes in „many-to-many relationship (suppliers / producers /

distributors) and application of shared communication tools and execution of purchase-sales processes.

Example: Tenders and auctions on web platforms (e-marketplace) enabling many competitive suppliers to sell to many competitive producers. Wide use of VMI and CPFR systems.

When considering which model is to be a target one for a given organization in a shorter or longer time horizon, as the next step it is worth to determine who should manage this area.

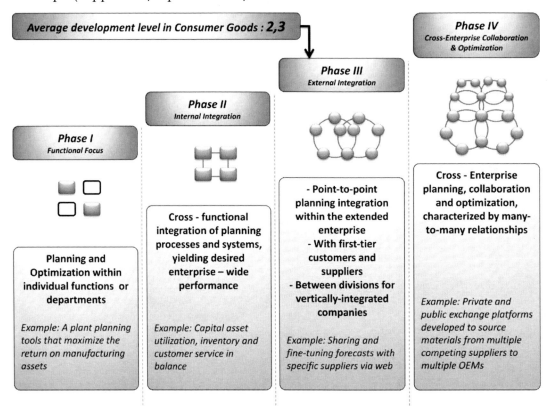

Figure 23- Development stages of the forecasting and SOP function

Location at the organization

To begin this section let us look at some statistics. According to the findings of the survey conducted by the Institute of Business Forecasting & Planning (IBFP), dealing in business forecasting, the forecasting function is located within the following organizational divisions[2]:

- *in 21% of cases in the Operations and Production divisions,*
- *in 20% of cases in the Marketing divisions,*
- *in 14% of cases in the Financial divisions,*
- *in 13% of cases in the Sales divisions*
- *in 10% of cases in the dedicated Forecasting divisions,*
- *in 9% of cases in the Logistics divisions,*
- *in 5% of cases in the Strategic Planning divisions,*
- *in 8% of cases in the Other divisions.*

This brings us to the question: how do we know which division of the given organization should accommodate the forecasting function? Or in other words: which premises should we follow when taking a decision on location of the forecasting function within the organization?

The data above could be used as a certain hint, however, we should remember that it should be a division which:

- manages the process and offers **one forecast for all** the company divisions involved,
- **cooperates with the stakeholders in the process within the organization**, i.e.

Sales, Marketing, Production, Purchasing, Logistics, Management Board,
- **cooperates with the external stakeholders** in the process (i.e. Contractors, Distributors, Customers).

However, when trying to answer the question asked earlier, where *to place* the forecasting function, we should honestly answer *…IT DEPENDS…!*

The decision where within the organization to create a unit responsible for a process of forecasting, should be based on the following premises, indicating the staff of this division of the company who:

1. have naturally the **fullest and fastest access to** all the **current information required for forecasting**,
2. have the **best knowledge of the market** and its operating mechanisms, i.e. the trends, dependencies, the rate and scale of changes, etc.

The decision on who within the organization will be responsible for forecasting is one of the strategic decisions of the company as with high responsibility for the financial condition of the organization (directly) there come the discretions that enable control of planning in key areas of the organization.

Therefore, such decision should be well thought through and guarantee neutrality of opinions and balancing future forecasts.

Presented below[3] is location of the forecasting function depending on the industry. This list may be useful as reference when taking this important decision.

---

[2] after averaging the results for various industry branches / Jain (2004) IBF Survey

[3] Jain (2004) IBF Survey

Statistics for various industries in relation to embed the function of forecasting in the specific divisions:

- **Telecom Technologies**: *Forecasts Department - 28%, Financial Department - 18%, Operations and Production Department - 15%, Logistics Department - 10%, Marketing Department - 10%, Sales Department - 8%, Strategic Planning Department - 8%, Other - 2%;*
- **Retail Trade**: *Sales Department - 21%, Operations and Production Department - 21%, Marketing Department - 11%, Logistics Department - 8%, Forecasts Department - 8%, Strategic Planning Department - 8%, Financial Department - 8%, Other- 15%;*
- **Pharmaceutical Industry**: *Marketing Department - 40%, Operations and Production Department - 15%, Forecasts Department - 14%, Logistics Department - 7%, Strategic Planning Department - 7%, Financial Department - 7%, Sales Department - 3%, Other - 7%;*
- **Industrial Production**: *Sales Department - 17%, Marketing Department - 15%, Operations and Production Department - 15%, Financial Department - 15%, Strategic Planning Department - 12%, Logistics Department - 8%, Forecasts Department - 5%, Other - 13%;*
- **Healthcare**: *Marketing Department - 22%, Logistics Department - 22%, Operations and Production Department - 15%, Sales Department - 10%, Financial Department - 7%, Forecasts Department - 6%, Strategic Planning Department - 4%, Other - 14%;*
- **Food and Beverage Production**: *Marketing Department - 20%, Operations and Production Department- 20%, Logistics Department - 18%, Sales Department - 15%, Forecasts Department - 10%, Financial Department - 9%, Strategic Planning Department - 2%, Other - 6%;*
- **Consumer Goods**: *Operations and Production Department - 25%, Sales Department - 16%, Marketing Department - 15%, Financial Department - 13%, Logistics Department - 12%, Forecasts Department - 9%, Strategic Planning Department - 3%, Other - 7%;*
- **New Technologies / IT**: *Marketing Department - 25%, Sales Department - 16%, Operations and Production Department - 16%, Forecasts Department - 14%, Logistics Department - 12%, Financial Department - 12%, Strategic Planning Department - 2%, Other - 3%;*
- **Automotive**: *Operations and Production Department - 29%, Marketing Department - 22%, Logistics Department - 20%, Sales Department - 8%, Strategic Planning Department - 4%, Financial Department - 2%, Forecasts Department - 2%, Other - 13%).*

Optimum Team Number

As a standard, it is accepted that the optimum number of staff on the team responsible for forecasting sales is from 2 to 4 people plus the manager. And this is the usual number of members of the forecasting teams.

The number of people on the team, needed to offer high level forecasts, is nevertheless related to several factors. Firstly it depends on the amount of work that the team must perform and the workload (no surprise) depends on:

• number of products (independent indices) subject to forecasting, and

• complexity of the forecasting process – in other words, how many of those indices are easy to forecast and how many require longer analyses, consultations and arrangements).

It is generally assumed that 1 person on

the team should be responsible for forecasting for 350-550 separate products (indices) which are sold in one, consistent sales regions (the same economic conditions, similar target group → the same product may be selling differently in Europe and completely differently in Asia or Africa). The top limit is adopted for the portfolio of relatively stable and reliable products, while the bottom limit is when the product sales is unstable, i.e. the sales is generated by promotional sales, marketing campaigns, short life-cycle products and many novelties introduced to the market (both own and competition's new products).

The XYZ analysis, discussed in more detail further on, shows which products represent the company's portfolio, in the context of complexity of forecasting.

A certain help may be provided by the findings of the survey[4] on the forecasting team numbers:

> *Average number of staff (FTEs) on the team responsible for forecasting in various industries:*
> - *retail sales - 5.4*
> - *pharmaceutical industry - 5.3*
> - *car industry - 5.1*
> - *healthcare - 5.0*
> - *IT - 4.8*
> - *consumer goods - 4.8*
> - *telecom - 4.8*
> - *food and beverage - 4.6*
> - *industrial products - 3.6*

As the above shows, the average team number is 5 FTEs including the manager.

---

[4] Jain (2004) IBF Survey

Key Discretions and Assignment of Tasks

The most important tasks of the forecasting team – apart from the general ones referred to earlier – include:

1. **Development of forecasts** via:
   a. generating **base statistical forecasts** (using the known methods, models and available systems supporting statistical forecasting),
   b. adding elements related to promotional sales, marketing campaign, introduction of **new products**, etc. → in others words the elements which could not be otherwise implemented in the forecasting models generating the base (statistical) forecast,
   c. and managing the process so as to work out the **consensus** as to the final forecast, together with all the involved stakeholders of the process.
2. Skillfully **persuading** the recipients about the **forecast reliability**; it is by no means about being able to explain the way out of forecast errors (unavoidable in any case), but to gain trust and justification of reliability of those forecasts on the basis of the best available knowledge and involvement of the process stakeholders.
3. Taking efforts in order to **continually improve forecasting quality** both in the context of methods, tools and the process itself.

On the basis of these tasks it is possible to determine which competences should the dedicated team have.

It is clear that one of the most important competences are widely understood analytical skills, and to be more precise:

- knowledge of mathematics, and especially at minimum good knowledge of statistics and understanding forecasting methods,
- understanding the meaning of processed numbers, calculated errors, generated statistics and the related implications in the context of business.

Another key competence is ability to swiftly use IT skills as:

- usually the challenge lies in quick and mass data processing (when we forecast on the level of SKU or index) and then the ability to automate these tasks using the available tools allow to lower the stress induced by working under time pressure; therefore good knowledge and certain creativity when selecting appropriate tools is definitely an important asset,
- it is needed to automate corrections and reviews of forecasts generated in systems supporting statistical forecasting, and then transferred to the ERP systems.

Another important competence are well developed **interpersonal and communication skills** which allow to:

- easily communicate across all levels of organization (regardless of the performed function and place in the hierarchy), with individuals who have information and knowledge regarding demand and sales, soliciting this information and acquiring it,
- communicate with all the process stakeholders (from the commercial and operational areas and the management board) in order to consult, review and accept the forecasts.

It is also clear that the team must have a thorough **understanding of business**, meaning:

- awareness of changes in the demand and

what is the reason for those changes,

- ability to identify and understand the developing market trends, seasonality and purchase cycles in specific regions, sales channels, customers, etc.,
- ability to specify which market information is important to the forecasting process (from Marketing, Sales, Production, Strategic Planning areas), as well as
- ability to decide which statistical forecasts and in which circumstances require correction using expert methods.

Another important competence, especially for the manager of the department or the process owner is the **ability to manage the process**, which:

- ensures that the company works out one consistent forecast which applies to all the departments of the organization → a goal of many companies and at the same time the best business practice,
- enables fruitful cooperation with staff in other company areas (consultations) in order to prepare a common forecast (→ consensus),
- enables holding and moderating meetings in a way that increases their effectiveness, development and reporting the achieved results (forecasts, deviations and their reasons), etc.

Many managers, after getting to know the aforesaid requirements as to the competences may say that this is a dream team and can only be created on paper. Especially when we think about combining within one person strong analytical and computer skills with highly developed communication and interpersonal skills.

Being fully aware of the general perception of analysts as hidden behind computers and crunching numbers, hoping nobody will call them out, and knowing how hard it is to imagine these people as charismatic crowd leaders, public speakers, able to bring everyone at the company to follow everything worked out in teams with people whom they might have not even known before.

There really exist people with such competences and areas which fall short may definitely be improved. All it takes is taking a good look at the company staff to identify such individuals. This requires good people skills and managerial attention and this effort pays off.

Presented below are results of the conducted research[5], showing the respective company areas from which the sales forecasting team members are recruited.

Research shows that forecasting specialists and managers are recruited from the following company departments respectively:

- *the highest number, **23%**, is recruited from **Marketing / Product Management** areas*
- ***19%** from **Production, Logistics, Distribution***
- ***16%** from **Analytical** areas*
- ***14%** from **Accounting** and **Finance** areas*
- ***11%** from **Sales***
- ***7%** from **Marketing Research***
- ***6%** from **IT** and **Technical Support***
- ***4%** from other areas*

This data shows that there is no one *best source* of people for the sales forecasting team. A conclusion may also be drawn that possessing strictly analytical skills does not determine the person's forecasting abilities.

When building a forecasting team, it is vital to ask the following question: should

---

[5] Jain (2003) Benchmarking Forecasting Practices, New York

the entire team have all the required competences and how to assign tasks within the team?

With regard to the statistical forecasting tasks, every team member should be responsible for a product range.

The assignment of tasks does not necessarily need to be equal in terms of numbers. It is important to optimally use the specific skills and abilities of individual team members and execute the department's deliverables in this manner. Therefore the forecasting products may be assigned according to:

- **sales channel** (key customers / segments, e.g. wholesale – retail),
- product line / category / family,
- **geographical region** (e.g. all the products and distribution channels in a given region / country / continent),
- product **sales specifics**; i.e. if there are product groups that are important for business such as products that are sold regularly, promotionally / on impulse, cyclically newly introduced, seasonal, then it is possible to assign those product groups to the persons who will develop forecasts for those products more easily. Thus, the computer savvy will easily support the regularly sold mass products,

while the negotiator type will faster and easier obtain the knowledge, required for forecasting of promotional sales or sales of newly launched products, from the sales forces or customers. The methodology wizard, on the other hand, will more effectively identify phenomena, trends, seasonality and will apply optimal model and parameters.

In justified cases it may be reasonable to combine the aforesaid approaches.

Assignment of discretion levels to individuals within the teams also depends on the specifics of a given company, i.e. how it is organized and divided into business units. It does not make sense to create another, artificial, division of products for the purposes of the forecasting process (as somebody said so or wrote so), completely removed from reality of the company. The suggestion is to rather optimally prepare the team and assign the tasks according to the company's business environment. The other tasks of the department, not related to generating forecasts, may be adjusted according to individual abilities, skills and personalities of team members. This lies within the discretion of the team manager and his/her managerial repertoire.

Challenges

As it is easily noticed, the department's tasks, other than forecasting, boil down to cooperation and coordination of operations of majority of key departments of the company and the related challenges faced by the team are also interdisciplinary. Some of them are briefly discussed below.

Forecasting and Planning Pluralism

As it has already been noted earlier, one of the main challenges of the forecasting department, regardless of its position within the organization, is to achieve the situation when there is one sales forecast for the purposes of all the departments. This means that operational planning (sales, production, purchase, distribution) and financial plans (e.g. cash flow) will be rooted in only one forecast. If it is modified upon a request of one of the stakeholders, it will be understood that such change will be reflected in all the other plans.

This issue should not be limited only to short-term forecasting. The department should be responsible for creating or at least co-creating the sales forecasts 4-12 months in advance (medium term forecasts) and over 12 months (long-term forecasts).

One number forecast should not be mistaken for the practice of variant planning which is used in the conditions of unstable markets, high competitiveness, lack of or suspended strategic decisions of the management board or the owners. One number forecast basically means that at any given moment one version of the sales forecast is in effect and applicable.

Although it seems obvious that every company aims to achieve such goal (and it is a desired business practice), survey[6] shows that less than 60% of companies practice one version of the sales forecast. Therefore, it is by no means an unimportant matter.

---

[6] Jain (2004) IBF Survey

Divergent Departmental Interests

Creating multiple versions of forecasts across the departments is justifiable as there are different departmental interests. What does it mean? As it has already been described in the introductory section, after each of the key departments of the company has developed the sales forecasts (both the Sales, Marketing and the Production, Purchasing and Finance departments – with the sales forecast by each of those departments it usually turned out that these forecasts are not only not convergent with one another but in many cases very remote indeed.

There are in fact two main reasons for this situation:

1. it is clear that there is no equal access to information that influences the forecast or that there is different awareness within the departments as to the factors vital to producing the forecast.
2. there has existed and still exists an additional factor which purposefully distorts the sales forecast, and it is related to the specific interests of individual departments.

What does the term *'distort'* mean as used above? Each department has its specific goals which it is accountable for or subject to bonus.

In general, the Sales Departments prefer underestimated forecasts as they are usually expected to deliver on the sales volumes (quantity/value) and they are awarded an additional bonus for performance exceeding the plan.

It is clear that this approach is in conflict with the objectives of operations departments (Production, Purchasing) which are held accountable for ensuring the products are ready for sale (they are in a way 'punished' for causing stock shortage and unsatisfactory level of customer service), and therefore they prefer to overestimated their forecasts.

Marketing Departments generally also show a tendency to overestimate forecasts as marketing budgets are derived from the declared sales volume and it is clear that whenever there is a higher budget available, it is possible to deliver the individual marketing goals (market shares, consumer awareness level, distribution level, etc.), subject to bonus, using less effort.

It is unfortunately a disadvantageous phenomenon for companies as a lot of time is used at meetings of heads of departments or management boards, to justify each version of the forecast/plan and bring them to one platform so as to be able to take the appropriate managerial decisions. It is important to be aware all the while that the time of those people at the organization is exceptionally expensive. There is no need to repeat arguments described in the earlier section discussing the importance of forecasting in business.

Even where there is a one forecast version at the organization, this aspect will pose challenge for the team, which will be submitted to manipulations and temptations from the interested and involved departments.

It is clear that this is a frequently encountered problem as we look at the survey[7] where 50% of respondents mentioned this problem existed at their organizations.

Executive Support

The intention of indicating the executive support is to draw attention of the senior executives to the fact that their support is necessary for the process to continue.

Furthermore, it is also important to assume that at the senior executive level there is awareness of the challenges mentioned in the earlier subsections.

Experience shows that even the most autonomous and well settled forecasting department cannot face the challenges, especially at the process implementation stage, without the support of senior executives. Hence, it is vital to make the executive boards pay attention to accuracy of implementation and then the appropriate functioning of the process and efficient management by the dedicated team (whether it handles the challenges well). Although it is hard to expect open complaints about insubordination of the other process participants, the opportunity to exchange notes on performance of the process may arise during meetings of the process leader with the Executive Board as part of the forecasting cycle, as discussed in the next section.

In the surveyed[8] companies, 50% of respondents declare a lot of support from the executive personnel, while 45% evaluate it as noticeable.

Incentive system

The incentive system related to forecasting quality is one of the more controversial elements of the process

---

[7] Jain (2004) IBF Survey

[8] Jain (2004) IBF Survey

support. Nevertheless, it is introduced in order to motivate all the process participants to commit to constant improvement of quality of the generated forecasts.

One may ask *'Who should be included in the system?'* but considering the above it should include everyone involved in the process. It is extremely important that it covers the participants who provide key information during the forecasting process (sales, marketing, market research etc.)

It needs to be considered that the system must provide an incentive so not just punish for the mistakes but also reward the achieved forecast quality improvement results. Therefore, from the point of view of the incentive system, the forecasting leader should be responsible for quality of forecasts as a whole, whereas the individual team members should be responsible for the parts of those forecasts that correspond to their respective areas (market / product group).

Similarly, responsibility for the forecasts in the context of the incentive system should be assigned to individual sales teams, especially if the main sales mechanisms are promotional activities, e.g. the head of the retail channel is responsible for the forecast quality in this channel, while the head of the wholesale channel for the respective forecast quality in the wholesale channel.

If the sales is strongly driven by marketing campaigns, the incentive system should include the manager responsible for the campaign for a specific product group. Similarly, if the marketing department is successively bringing new products into the market, it should be included in the incentive system within the scope of new product development (NPD) at the very least.

Therefore, the incentive system should not be there to *complicate life* of the employees who in fact have no influence over it or any influence they have is limited. Hence, it is not recommended for such system to include the sales representatives (e.g. on the FMCG market) although it may be warranted to include the heads of channels or regions where the sales representatives are employed.

An appropriately shaped incentive system may prove to be an efficient tool eliminating any impulses to enforce interests of individual departments.

An important question is how to measure quality of forecasts for the purposes of the incentive system. It will be discussed in more detail in one of the subsequent chapters (6. Forecasting Quality Measurement, page 141). At this moment it suffice it to say that:

- for the purposes of the incentive system it is crucial to measure forecast quality over the time horizon which is justified by business requirements, i.e. when any forecast change allows for rescheduling of the supplies chain (production/deliveries schedules) so that the demand arising from such a changed forecast can be realistically met after the changes introduced to the operational planning,
- it is beneficial to report forecast quality in cumulative terms, i.e. quality is measured so that at the end of each month the report shows the value from the year beginning to the end of the past month; thus allowing to objectively assess the current quality level and measure any progress,
- it is important for the forecast quality reporting system to enable ongoing reporting on every element (market x product) necessary to evaluate the forecast quality from the point of view of every participant, e.g. the aforementioned channel leaders, marketing managers, etc.

Position in the Organizational Hierarchy

Upon reading the previous chapters of this book it comes to mind that the position of the forecasting team in the organizational hierarchy is not as important as who is on the team and who manages it.

Nevertheless, it is good practice to position such team within the organization so as to offer it quick and easy access to key information which affects the forecasts.

Hence, for companies with complex sales force structure, where such sales forces act as a kind of *market information bureau* picking up market movements, trends, competition's activities, etc., the forecasting team is usually positioned within the sales department. Whenever fast communication with suppliers is required – it is placed within the operational structures, etc.

It is hard to determine one solution as better than others for it is dependent on the business specifics, internal relations, communications culture within a given organization and other aspects that determine a flow of more or less formal information which aids the forecasting process.

Wrapping up, while discussing the position of such unit in any organization it must be stressed that when it is already placed within the structure it should be appropriately positioned in the organizational hierarchy. Foremostly it is important that the person in charge of the process and the team is on the same hierarchical level as the heads of the involved departments whose forecasting activities are coordinated by that person. The image and status of that individual in the organization should be clearly comparable to that of the partners from other departments.

Similarly, the sales forecasting team is not a team of analysts, the chart-makers, but a team which is to a great extent responsible for optimization of the supplies chain and – as indicated when speaking of the importance of that process – many time a multimillion profits or losses for the company. It is therefore important to take care of such dream team's, once created, image and motivation.

Chairing of SOP meetings

The meeting's leader and moderator is usually – as the process owner – the head of the forecasting department or a team member appointed by the process owner. Organization and holding of such meetings is an important task as it is the process element that requires all the decision making persons from the departments involved to meet at one time and agree ONE COMMON FORECAST.

This is a real challenge due to the following factors:

1. The meeting must take place on a scheduled date each month (if the month is a cycle and it usually is) with a tolerance of +/- 3 days; although it is a cyclical meeting, all the participants should be aware of its priority and if such awareness is missing the forecasting department must build it.

2. Another part of the challenge is that the decision-making persons from the departments involved are available. Since the meeting is aimed at producing a common forecast decision, it should only be attended by the decision-making persons who are prepared to it, e.g. who have the initial forecast information at hand and know how their respective

areas work; they are also authorized to take decision regarding the processes in their respective area. If these are not heads of the departments, they may be in exceptional situation represented by the persons formally authorized to take decision in their stead during such meeting; situations like this naturally arise due to holiday or sick leaves or other fortuitous events.

3. Finally, there is the last element of the challenge, namely time and place where the particular interests of the departments are confronted. The meeting's chairman cannot allow for a situation where the developed forecast is biased and unreasonably favours the interests of one of the departments involved because all the process participants could not meet at a set time and place. Every forecast review should be justified and approved by all the process participants involved.

The details pertaining to such a valid process event have been set out in a more specific way in the next chapter on organization and management of the forecasting process. Research[9] shows that such meetings are held in 80% of the surveyed companies.

---

[9] Jain (2004) IBF Survey

SUMMARY

- When building a forecasting team in the organization one must keep in mind which forecasting model we are interested in (process integration only internal or also external),
- Forecasting team, depending on the industry, may be placed in various parts within the organization's structure - what is important is an easy access (less or more formal) to all the information required for forecasting,
- The team's size depends on the number of products and the level of their complexity with regard to forecasting (how difficult they are to forecast, using the XYZ analysis),
- The scope of discretion required for execution of the forecasting process is wide and it requires constant development of this personnel,
- Challenges for this department, and foremostly its leader, are challenges for the top executives who should support it,
- An important success factor for the forecasting process is implementation of the incentive system for the managers involved in the process, connected with quality of the forecasts which they have co-created,
- It is more important to appropriately fix the department and its leader within the organization's hierarchy than within its structure.

4. Sales Forecasting Process

This chapter discusses:
- analysis which allows to optimally use the time and the team to forecast individual product   groups,
- integration of the forecasting process with key areas of contemporary business,
- how to organize an optimal forecasting and planning cycle, namely how to combine elements of the forecasting process to cohere as a whole,
- how to automate the process of forecasting.

Preparation for process implementation and management

This chapter presents an approach to the forecasting process which allows to save time and resources, mostly the human ones. This approach employs the following assumptions:

1. not all the products require the same amount of time, and generally the resources, so as to achieve a satisfactory, from business point of view, forecast quality,
2. similar level of forecast quality for a number of different products does not bring the company similar business results.

This thesis does not require a proof and it is not a purpose of this publication. Nevertheless, suffice it to refer to Pareto's law which deals with uneven distribution of most things in life, and in most popular version it explains that 80% of the result is generated by 20% of the causes, i.e.:

- 20% of the goods generate 80% of the revenue,
- 20% of the goods generate 80% of the production costs,
- 20% of customers create 80% of the turnover,

etc.

Forecast Elements

Before we start segmentation of the offer, which we will forecast according to the resource consumption criteria, we need to be aware of the components of the sales and, in turn, its forecast. Usually not all those components are present at one time.

Basically if we consider the sales and its forecast we must be aware that the forecast volume is generally a sum total of **three components** driven by the specific sales process in a given company or on a given market:

1. the **BASIC** (also referred to as regular) sales forecast which is easiest to predict, shows regularity and fundamentally can be forecast using simple statistical (objective) methods, i.e. can be described using mathematic formulas and simple heuristics,

2. **PROMOTIONAL** sales forecast which is a result of the scheduled (and generally non repetitive) actions supporting the basic sales; in relation to the market realities, such activities may involve:
   a. offering a cash discount by the customer relationship manager for purchase of the prearranged goods in a specific amount (apart from standard trading terms but within the planned marketing budget),
   b. offering a discount in kind, i.e. providing the customer with additional goods at much lower prices than provided for in standard relationship agreement, once the customer exceeds the agreed purchase volume over a specific time horizon,
   c. supporting the sales with various marketing and media campaigns – so called ATL (*Above The Line*), i.e. TV, radio, outdoor advertising, Internet, etc.,

usually prepared and financed by the marketing department,

d. supporting the sales with Trade Marketing – BTL (*Below The Line*) or TTL (*Through The Line*),

e. running loyalty schemes,

f. conducting various other forms of influencing the customers' and consumers' decisions at a specific time.

Sometimes such activities are run cyclically at specific seasons. Assuming that their cyclicality is maintained they may be treated as seasonal sales (e.g. pre-Xmas sale). The decision on how to treat such sales and also the optimal forecasting method to pick is taken by the person in charge of forecasting.

Usually the structural analogy methods or other expert methods are applied to forecast such component.

3. The **NPD** (*New Product Development*) sales forecast, namely the forecast component which involves introduction of new products to sales. Development of such sales is usually forecast by the department in charge of launching new products on the market and it usually is the marketing department. Subject to the market specifics, it may be assumed that the phase when the product may be treated as a new product lasts from 6 to 12 month. It is good practice that forecasting for the new products be in that department that brings them to the market (usually marketing or R&D department) and which refers such forecasts to the forecasting department. There are several arguments for such solution:

a. foremostly it is the department responsible for a new product launch that formulates the predictions regarding its sales over subsequent periods of its introduction,

b. this department monitors whether the

sales is growing over time as predicted,

c. the new product market launch is usually accompanied by a strong marketing and promotional support whose insensitivity is adjusted to the needs, most often determined by the launching department.

It is possible, however, to leave responsibility for the NPD with the forecasting department, particularly in situations when we have access to large amounts of historical data on introduction of new products to the market where such products are similar and it is possible to use the structural analogies methods.

Let's be aware that in today's world:

- product shelf life is shorter than in the past (if nothing else because of their increasing innovation under the pressure of stronger competition and technological development),

- natural sales characteristics are very often modified by appropriately planned marketing and promotion activities which follow from strategy enforcement and are yet another argument for leaving responsibility for forecasting new products with the department launching them to the market.

What is important from the point of view of sales forecasting is that the aforesaid forecast components do not depend on the range of goods as such but on the stage of the product's life cycle and on whether its sales is stimulated from the outside and if yes, to what extent, or whether it is a reflection of a natural consumer demand.

The person in charge of forecasting should be aware of those components and their volatility over time as they determine methodologies to use so as to achieve an optimum forecast quality. This is because some methods are used for basic sales, other ones for promotional sales and still other ones for the NPD.

Summary: each product category may contain products with the aforesaid sales components, and it is the task of the person in charge of forecasting to recognize which of those are effective at a given time and which forecasting method should be therefore applied.

ABC Analysis of the Product Portfolio

The ABC analysis is one of the major analyses conducted by companies in respect of various types of resources (i.e. products, contractors. In case of product segmentation for the purposes of the forecasting process optimization it should be conducted as one of the first analyses and then cyclically updated.

This analysis concept is based on Pareto's law. Its result is the product portfolio (generally the range and goods and services offered) arranged in 3 groups:

1. **class A products** – top priority products for the company from the point of view of revenue or profit; they generate high revenue at a relatively low cost; these are the products sold in high volumes, characterized by high demand; the company cannot run without them;

2. **class B products** – not top priority but still important from the perspective of revenue or profit; these are usually the products that are being withdrawn from the market or just arriving without any certainty as to their future

sales; offering those products is not a priority in the sense of securing the company's future, nevertheless, they must be in the portfolio from the point of view of strategy or streamlining of operations;

3. **class C products** – the goods that are marginally important to the organization from the point of view of revenue or profits but they constitute a big group and generate substantial administrative expenses. As a result, the relation of revenue/profits to the related to expenditure is unfavourable and on many occasions these products turn out to be generating losses. In all honesty, from the perspective of the products' *'hygiene'*, majority of products classified in this group should be removed from the offer as soon as possible. This group includes both the products that are subject to withdrawal from the market and the NPD that areas only to reach a higher sales level but still, they should be constantly watched for whether their sales is developing as assumed – and if definitely no, they should be removed as soon as possible.

Based on such analysis we may start taking specific steps aimed at generating the results.

Firstly, we must determine which value will serve as a measure of the product's importance to the organization. This should be the data which can be quickly obtained from the accounting system, a transactional system (ERP) or calculated and which will reflect a value it represents for the company.

The importance criteria include for instance:

- sales volume,
- sales value,
- margin, etc.

As far as the importance criteria are concerned, the following aspects should be taken into account:

- the sales amount (volume) may be used if the margins across the offered range of goods are similar and the sales is executed without the promotion or if the promotion offer is similar across the offered range of goods,
- the sales value may be applied when the price per item varies greatly across the entire range of goods,
- the margin is used whenever the sales margins for specific product groups are largely varied or when the sales support politics for various product groups are strongly differentiated; applying the margin (e.g. MI / MII / MIII) as criteria depends on the type of promotional support while it is clear that MI margin calculation is much less complicated than MII margin (usually calculated several times a year in order to show the financial results).

In order to maintain objectivity of the conducted analysis, the data used should be the moving average, best for the last 12 months. It is even better to assume average values for the last 12 months - so that the data is comparative, i.e. it is possible to compare the product sold throughout the last year to the new

product on offer for only a couple of months.

Once we have picked a value representative as the importance criterion we can conduct the ABC analysis which boils down to the following steps:

1. arranging the goods in a descending order of importance (from the most important to the least important),
2. cumulating product importance ratios in the list of stock items in a descending order of importance and referring such cumulative ratio to the sum total for that ratio across the entire stock; thus, for every product in the arranged list, we arrive at a cumulative percentage which is a ratio of the increasing value e.g. the sales to the total value, e.g. the sales of the entire stock;
3. based on the percentage break for A, B and C classes, we check which products show the cumulative importance criteria for A, B and C classes; usually it is assumed that the percentage break between A and B class is 80%, and between B and C class it is 95%.

Example of the application of the ABC analysis is illustrated below (Figure 24).

As a result of correctly performed ABC analysis we obtain the structural knowledge of how individual products 'work' for the company, i.e. which are most valuable and which are the least valuable, and hence which should be forecast with utmost care and diligence during and which do not require such attention during the forecasting process.

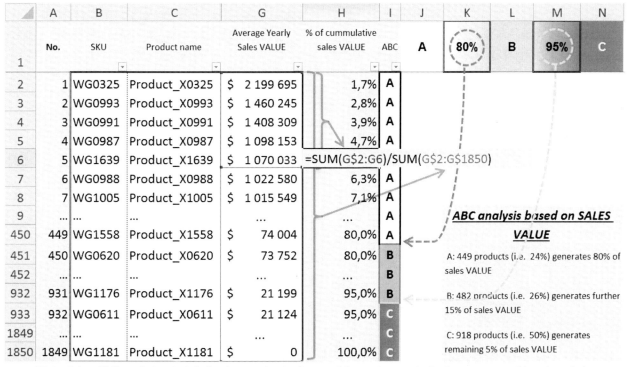

Figure 24 - ABC analysis principle (implementation in the spreadsheet using as criteria the average monthly sales value)

XYZ Analysis

Another analysis preparing for implementation of the forecasting process is an XYZ analysis which allows to segment the stock in 3 groups subject to difficulty (complexity) of forecasting:

1. **X class products** – relatively easy to forecast using formal methods,
2. **Y class products** – medium difficulty in forecasting using formal methods,
3. **Z class products** – hard to forecast using formal methods.

There are several methods of classifying products using this analysis. The first one involves the assessment of continuity of time series:

1. **X category**: products which are in a regular offer, characterized by a strong

demand and generally not offered on sale,
2. **Z category**: products characterized by very strong fluctuations in demand, requiring constant attention and consultation of the demand with Marketing, Sales Forces, Key Accounts, etc.
3. **Y category**: medium products falling outside X and X clusters (often in this category there are products that are trend sensitive or seasonal).

Another method of classifying products under the XYZ analysis is **examination of the standard variation** for the time series of the product's sales for the last 24-36 months (the period represented for the sales behavior assessment in the present stage of the product's life cycle):

1. **X category**: products which represent a stable level of sales, characterized by small fluctuations and regular demand, with a standard fluctuation rate in the monthly sales data **< 20%**,
2. **Y category**: products whose sales level shows much greater fluctuations but the sales are still regular; fluctuations (standard variation) in the sales are respectively **20-50%**,
3. **Z category**: products characterized by very high fluctuations and irregular sales; the standard fluctuation rate is respectively in **excess of 50%**, and the sales are clearly irregular (may be dwindling for most time).

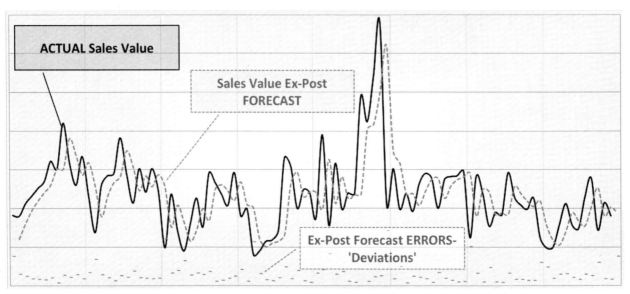

ACTUAL Sales Value

Sales Value Ex-Post FORECAST

Ex-Post Forecast ERRORS-'Deviations'

Figure 25 - Ex-post forecasting results vs. the actual sales and forecast errors

Another classification method used as part of the XYZ analysis is **analysis of ex-post errors** in forecasts. This method boils down to generating ex-post forecasts (Figure 25 above) for all the products in the portfolio, assuming that optimum forecast models and their parameters have been selected (5. *Forecasting Methodologies and Models*, page 97), and then calculation of the forecast error (6. *Forecasting Quality Measurement*, page 141) for a representative period (e.g. 12 months). After the appropriate calculations have been performed we arrive at a set of averages for the forecast errors, allocated to the individual products. We divide such set of errors into 3 ranges corresponding to individual categories, most often according to the following criteria:

1. **X category**: error products represent **<15%**,
2. **Y category**: error products represent **15-25%**,
3. **Z category**: error products represent **>25%**,

where the percentage break determining a specific category depends on the industry and market specifics, qualitative ratios set as goals for the forecasting process and other internal conditions. If there is standard error distribution, statistical distribution methods may be used, Pareto's Law, etc.

At this stage, the most important fact is that the result of this analysis is portfolio of products segmented according to the objective criterion of the forecasting difficulty. Thus, apart from the importance criterion (ABC) each product may have the XYZ complexity criterion allocated to it, resulting in a product table similar to that presented in Figure 26 below.

	A	C	D	E	I	J	K
1	No.	XYZ	SKU	Product name	Average Yearly Sales VALUE	% of cummulative sales VALUE	ABC
2	1	Z	WG0325	Product_X0325	$2 199 695	1,7%	A
3	2	Z	WG0993	Product_X0993	$1 460 245	2,8%	A
4	3	Z	WG0991	Product_X0991	$1 408 309	3,9%	A
5	4	Z	WG0987	Product_X0987	$1 098 153	4,7%	A
6	5	X	WG1639	Product_X1639	$1 070 033	5,5%	A
7	6	X	WG0988	Product_X0988	$1 022 580	6,3%	A
8	7	Z	WG1005	Product_X1005	$1 015 549	7,1%	A
9	...	...	...	...	...	...	A
450	449	Y	WG1558	Product_X1558	$74 004	80,0%	A
451	450	Z	WG0620	Product_X0620	$73 752	80,0%	B
452	...	...	...	...	...	...	B
932	931	Z	WG1176	Product_X1176	$21 199	95,0%	B
933	932	X	WG0611	Product_X0611	$21 124	95,0%	C
1849	...	...	...	...	...	...	C
1850	1849	Y	WG1181	Product_X1181	$0	100,0%	C

Figure 26 - List of products with ABC and XYZ parameters

Additional Process Control Parameters

In the business reality there are often still other process control parameters of products that are used. In such situations the parameters must also be linked to the forecasting process.

One of such additional, frequently used parameters is the product life cycle (PLC) which may adopt the following values:

- **N** – new products
- **R** – regular offer products
- **W** – products subject to withdrawal

As both the regular offer products and those subject to withdrawal are usually the products with history and the assigned forecasting models, for the purposes of forecasting it is usually sufficient to classify them according to the importance criteria (ABC). In case of new products, however, the situation is that much more complicated as the forecasting team cannot predict them due to no sales history. Usually, at this stage of the product life cycle forecasting is coordinated by the department launching the product on the market (i.e. Marketing, R&D). In such situations it is often a practice to create another category on top of the ABC analysis result, so that there are not 3 but 4 categories of importance **ABC+N** (although the semantics are slightly different here).

Another product characteristic used to control the product in business processes is the ratio that defines **quantity of recipients** (especially for the purposes of operational planning). The so called STU classification is introduced and the following 3 product categories are set:

- **S** (Single) – product which in the entire customer portfolio of the company has only **1 recipient**,
- **T** (Triple) – product which is sold to a **small group** of customers, as a standard up to 3 but it is possible to allow 5, 10 or even more – it depends on the total number of customers,
- **U** (Universal) – products which are universal and **mass sold** to a wide group of customers.

The specified product characteristics, if used, are also appropriately integrated and used in the forecasting process and any related operational planning.

Process Management Matrix

Having conducted the ABC and the XYZ analysis of the goods we get the list as specified in Figure 27 below.

Now every product is assigned to one of 9 classes, which is a result of the matrix for combination of characteristics which determine its importance (ABC) and complexity of forecasting (XYZ): AX, AY, AZ, BX, BY, BZ, CX, CY, CZ.

The meaning of assigning products to each of 9 classes is as follows:

- **AX** – products of high value to the company, characterized by regular, predictable sales, easy to forecast,
- **AY** – also products of high value to the company but their sales are characterized by certain fluctuations – nevertheless they are still rather regular so the products are characterized by *medium level* of difficulty of forecasting,
- **AZ** are also products very valuable to the company but due to their highly irregular sales they are very hard and time consuming to forecast,
- **BX** are products whose importance to the company is secondary but they are easy to forecast and characterized by rather regular sales,
- **BY** are also secondary products in the portfolio but showing certain irregularities in time series, i.e. medium level of forecasting difficulty,
- **BZ** are also products of secondary importance to the company but their forecasting is hard and time consuming as they show very irregular sales history,
- **CX** are products of the least importance to the company but easily forecast,
- **CY** are products of little importance to the company and additionally showing irregular sales over time,
- **CZ** are products that are insignificant and additionally characterized by irregular sales and thus very hard to forecast.

	B	C	D	E	I	J	K
	ABC x **XYZ**	XYZ	SKU	Product name	Average Yearly Sales VALUE	% of cummulative sales VALUE	ABC
1							
2	**AZ**	Z	WG0325	Product_X0325	$2 199 695	1,7%	A
3	**AZ**	Z	WG0993	Product_X0993	$1 460 245	2,8%	A
4	**AZ**	Z	WG0991	Product_X0991	$1 408 309	3,9%	A
5	**AZ**	Z	WG0987	Product_X0987	$1 098 153	4,7%	A
6	**AX**	X	WG1639	Product_X1639	$1 070 033	5,5%	A
7	**AX**	X	WG0988	Product_X0988	$1 022 580	6,3%	A
8	**AZ**	Z	WG1005	Product_X1005	$1 015 549	7,1%	A
9	...	...	...	...	...	...	A
450	**AY**	Y	WG1558	Product_X1558	$74 004	80,0%	A
451	**BZ**	Z	WG0620	Product_X0620	$73 752	80,0%	B
452	...	...	...	...	...	...	B
932	**BZ**	Z	WG1176	Product_X1176	$21 199	95,0%	B
933	**CX**	X	WG0611	Product_X0611	$21 124	95,0%	C
1849	...	...	...	...	...	...	C
1850	**CY**	Y	WG1181	Product_X1181	$0	100,0%	C
1851							

Figure 27 - Products listed according to ABC and XYZ parameters in a 2-dimensional matrix

The Figure 28 presents visualization of ABC-XYZ matrix, were Z axis indicates the number of products in a given class and the suggested approach to automation of forecasting. With the products segmented like this it is possible to take initial decisions on the selected methods and automation of forecasting and even if the general approach is shown by Figure 28, it should be completed to include the following comments:

1. **CX** class products:
   FULL AUTOMATION – due to low significance and high regularity of sales, it is usually subject to automatic forecasting using objective (statistical) methods, without reviewing them with expert (subjective) methods,

2. **BX-CY-CZ** class products:
   AUTOMATION WITH REGULAR CONTROL – these product groups are subject to automatic forecasting using statistical methods after first *history clearing* from the effects of irregular factors (i.e. promotional sales), and they verified using subjective methods, i.e. using the experts forum (Key Account Managers, Sales Managers, Product Managers, etc.),

3. **AX-AY-AZ-BY-BZ** class products:
   MAINLY SUBJECTIVE METHODS – these products are of key significance to

the organization but hard to forecast due to irregular and historically interrupted time series; although forecasts may be supported with statistical models probably as in the second group each product is individually reviewed at the expert forum with due diligence as these are usually the products where most of the trading volumes are generated by promotional, impulse or seasonal sales.

An exception are the AX class products which can be rather easily forecast using objective methods, nonetheless, considering their high importance to the organization (this rather small group of products may represent as much as 40-60% of the company's turnover!), even good quality forecasts should be consulted at the expert forum and verified using subjective methods.

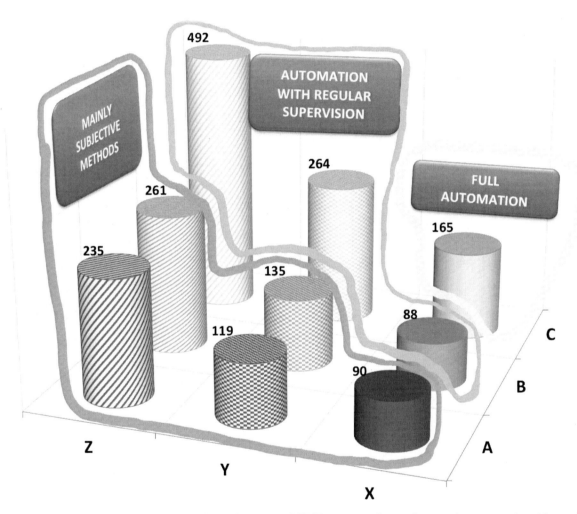

Figure 28 - Examples of products listed according to ABC-XYZ matrix and general approach to automation of forecasting

When the decisions regarding automation of individual product groups are made, it is worth to consider implementation of system alerts which under special circumstances

would notify the person in charge of forecasting of an extraordinary event (the so called exception) which may impact the forecast. Alerts could be sent as a result of the following events:

- the sales much higher or lower in the preceding month (in several months in a row) than assumed by the forecasts,
- change of the forecasting model, etc.

A well thought out system of alerts significantly relieves the team from constantly following the sales process and support ongoing improvement of the forecasting process, especially when there is a huge number of products for forecasting (from one thousand to several dozen of thousand indices) in the portfolio.

Forecasting Process

Automation Algorithm

At this stage, when as a result of the aforesaid analyses the products are selected for forecasting that can be automatically supported with objective methods, these methods need to be appropriately picked and the models adequately parameterized. This refers to products from 1,2 classes and AX products from class 3 (refer to *Process Management Matrix* chapter above). The following algorithm shows how to do this:

1. Select the lowest level of product aggregation for forecasting, adequate for your organization ($\rightarrow$ refer to the next chapter Forecasting Levels.),
2. For the selected forecasting level prepare and clear historic sales data for individual (classes) products:
   a. clear the sales history from the results of extraordinary sales (i.e. the impulse sales – so called outliers),
   b. smooth out the *'calendar effects'* (i.e. various holidays and days closed for business specific to a given country or market),

3. Prepare the basic forecasting models (refer to chapter *5. Forecasting Methodologies and Models*, page 97) with appropriately predefined parameters:
   a. Profile for **stationary series** for forecasting using Brown's Method ($\alpha=0.3$),
   b. Profile for **trend series** for forecasting using **Holt's Method** ($\alpha=0.3$, $\beta=0.05$),
   c. Profile for forecasting series with **seasonality effect** for forecasting using **Winter's Method** ($\alpha=0.3$, $\gamma=0.8$),
   d. Profile for forecasting **series with seasonality effect and trend** for forecasting using Holt-Winters ($\alpha=0.3$, $\beta=0.05$, $\gamma=0.8$),
4. Perform the analysis of time series for the selected products in the context of the sales process templates (stationary, with trend, with seasonality, with seasonality and trend) and assign appropriate forecasting model profiles,
5. Select the appropriate measures for monitoring quality of generated forecasts (refer to chapter *6. Forecasting Quality Measurement* page 141)
6. Develop a system of alerts which are automatically monitoring forecasting; such solution allows to quickly react to the noted anomalies or sudden or unexpected phenomena in the sales processes,
7. Increase the group of products that are forecast automatically using objective methods to include the ones that are more difficult (more complex) to forecast.
8. Successively increase the arsenal of forecasting methodology and models for automation; as you gain more experience and knowledge replace methods and models with more advanced (and more effective).

Forecasting Levels

At this stage of preparing the process, the decision has usually been already made as to which products will be subject to objective and which to subjective forecasts. Nonetheless, it has not been decided yet on which product hierarchy level the forecasting will be performed.

All truth be told, this section may seem to be coming a little late as considering the chronology such decision should be taken still before the ABC, XYZ analyses have been performed and the other characteristics for the goods subject to forecast been selected. Although such decision is taken by the managers based on their intuition, for better order the related issues should be identified and discussed.

This leads to a question: *On which level should forecasting be performed? SKU[10] ? Index ? Product? Product category? Brand?*

Again, the answer is ambiguous and it is safe: *IT DEPENDS.* And it does depend on the needs and abilities to obtain product information within the organization and outside the organization (contractors, research agencies, etc.). Answers to the following questions can aid the decision:

- On which level are market changes (trends, demand) noticeable the fastest?
- On which level is the information on sales promotion and competitive activities obtained?
- At which level are the marketing campaigns executed and how much 'down' in the hierarchy can their support be objectively divided into individual groups of products (product? Index? SKU?)
- At which level are the respective

[10] Stock-Keeping Unit

operations planned (mainly the production planning)?

In most cases of business practice forecasts are prepared on the index or product level. For a better understanding of this issue let's analyze this example:

- 'PARADISE FRUIT' drink is the product
- while indices for this product are the 'PARADISE FRUIT drink in:
  - 0.33l can
  - 0.5l plastic bottle
  - 1l plastic bottle
  - 1.5l carton

From the point of view of the production process it is more reasonable to use the product level as the know-how refers to the drink recipe, while packaging is secondary and is determined solely by a specific demand of individual sales channels and distribution networks.

However, from the point of view of sales channels management it is reasonable to forecast at the index level (can, bottle, carton) as production planning will still process the demand for various packaging types into demand for the drink expressed in liters and the demand for various raw materials and components, including an appropriate quantity of packaging in the form of cans, bottles, cartons. Thus, the forecasting should be based on the index level.

Bear in mind that notwithstanding accuracy of the forecasting level decision there is a principle regarding correspondence between the forecasting level and the quality of forecasts:

> There are **fewer forecasting errors** when we forecast at a **higher level of product** hierarchy. This is because the random sales mix-ups are compensated for when aggregated at higher levels.

Let's follow this principle on the example of beer sales. The same beer may be purchased by customers in the following packing types (indices):

- single 0.5l can
- 4-pack of 0.5l cans
- 6-pack of 0.5l cans
- single 0.33l bottle
- 4-pack of 0.33l bottles
- single 0.5l bottle

The forecast error, both for the can 6-pack and the other indices, will be much higher than the aggregate forecast of that beer sales expressed in liters, regardless of the packaging in which that beer was sold. This may stem from a simple fact that should one type of packaging be unavailable (as a result of unexpected demand in one region caused for instance by unforeseen heat) the customers will most probably purchase the same product but in different packaging as at the end of the day the consumer is looking for a specific brand and type of beer while the packaging is a secondary issue.

TOP-DOWN APPROCHING	BOTTOM-UP APPROCHING
PROS • Contain ready aggregated market information • Reflect strategy and plans • Incorporate macroeconomic factors	• Contain detailed local information and consumer information • Clearly indicate responsibility for forecasts and sales plans • ... and hence they provide more incentive
CONS • No assigned responsibility for the local sales agents, KAM • Introduces ambivalence between the notion of aggregated forecasts and the plans and targets • Motivated by the company's politics	• Aggregated forecasts may not be convergent with the plans • Hard to reconcile with the financial goals and the annual sales targets • May be false due to the sales targets • More resources (people and time) are required to generate them, which slows down the entire process

Figure 29 - PROs and CONs for TOP-DOWN and BOTTOM-UP approaches

Another important issue is the approach to defining the forecasting value at a detailed level and a general level. By and large the following two approaches are identified:

- **Bottom Up** where at first the lowest level forecasts are prepared (SKU, Index) and then they are aggregated to the top level via products → product groups → distribution channels → sales regions/geographic markets, etc.
- **Top-Down** where at first the global, top level forecast is prepared (e.g. for product categories across the entire organization) and then it is divided into individual brands, products, indices and SKU for the individual sales regions, distribution channels, customers and individual shops.

Each of these approaches is widely practiced and has its strengths and weaknesses. The list below shows the most important PROS and CONS for each approach. It is definitely worth reviewing them before we make a decision specific to every organization.

To summarize the forecasting level issue:

> **If possible, prepare your forecasts on the highest product hierarchy level but so as not to lose information which is important from the point of view of the departments involved.**

Forecasting horizons

Another important element during the process implementation stage is to set the time horizons which require the sales forecasts.

It is certainly possible to develop the forecasts for many horizons but nevertheless it is important to draw attention to the fact that calculation of the forecast quality, regular control, reporting and presenting are rather resource consuming activities both in the context of staff time involvement and the system's resources.

Thus it is suggested that analysis of needs and reduction of the forecasting horizons should be limited to a minimum that is justified from the business perspective.

Practice shows that the most important sales forecasting horizon is the one which – if there are any major changes to the forecasting level – the entire chain of supplies (purchases, production, logistics, distribution) is still – based on technological, operational and formal conditions – guarantee to customers such amount of products as required due to the changed forecast in this planning horizon. In such conditions the demand forecast still has a chance to remain sales forecast. In other words, it is the time horizon that guarantees flexible supply of goods via the supply chain. In the consumer goods[11] market it is usually 2-3 months.

Let's discuss an example which illustrates this issue. If in April we increase a demand forecast for X product over a **3-month horizon** (i.e. forecasting for July) by 100% (due to an unexpectedly increasing demand stemming from e.g. favorable weather conditions, withdrawal of the competitors' product from the market, etc.) then:

- the Production Department is still able to organize the resources necessary to produce a double amount of X without any harm to the forecasts of the other products,
- the Procurement Department can, on the other hand, based on the formal contracts, order any additional amounts of supplies, raw materials, components, without incurring excessive costs,
- the Logistics Department will also be able, without any excessive costs, procure and stock both the production resources and the ready goods.

However, if the Sales Department amends the forecast demand by the same amount (100%) but over the **horizon of 1 month** (forecasting for May), it rarely happens that:

- the Production Department is capable of providing the resources for double production at such short notice and even though there are solutions they entail additional and much higher costs,
- the Procurement and Logistics

---

[11] CG (Consumer Goods) or FMCG (Fast Moving Consumer Goods)

Department can ensure the supplies and raw materials for producing such additional amount of products, especially if the production requires specific materials and semi products which are shipped in by sea). The situation is complicated somewhat further if the forecast applies to ready goods produced for a given market in another part of the world (sourcing from OEM[12]).

In such circumstances, it is obvious that the sales forecast will vary from the demand forecast for a simple reason that it is not physically possible to ensure such additional amount of X product resulting from the changed demand forecast. The sales forecast may become realistic at a level which can be produced or supplied, subject to arrangements between all the parties concerned (Sales-Production-Logistics).

Going back then to the main thought: it is the forecast horizon, ensuring flexibility of production and the entire chain of supplies that should be adopted as basic for measurement of the forecast quality and for incentive schemes which account for the forecast quality.

What is more, we can cyclically prepare the so called auxiliary forecasts which contribute little in the context of operational and sales planning, however, they allow to take initial reviewing steps across the remaining business areas. These forecasts include:

- **M0 - current month forecast**: often referred to as the newest estimate or the Last Estimate which lends credence to execution of the sales plan in a given month or shows the most probable variations. This allows to prepare suggestions regarding reviews of the operational plans for subsequent months if such variations and important, usually it is prepared a few times per month,
- **M1 - next month forecast**: similarly to M0 forecast it is not possible to use it to offset certain valid changes of the demand forecasts, however, it is possible to review operational planning for the following periods on that basis,
- **M6 - 6-month forecast**: allows to review the sales forecast, even though it is most often used for reviews and arrangements pertaining to general contracts with the providers of supplies, raw materials, components, semi products and OEM; it is usually prepared at a higher level of the product hierarchy than the basic forecast (M2/M3), usually at the quarterly intervals,
- **M12 - annual forecast**: prepared on a higher level of product hierarchy and prepared in order to indicate medium- and long-term trends, allowing to develop the investment plans, financial projections and to review company's strategic plans and the related supporting activities; usually such forecast is prepared intensively at the end of each year as the basis for setting business and sales objectives for the next year – as a result the so called basic plan, annual target, the ZERO forecast is established.

To sum up and for order, Figure 30 below shows how various time horizons used in the sales forecasts are marked.

[12] Original Equipment Manufacturer

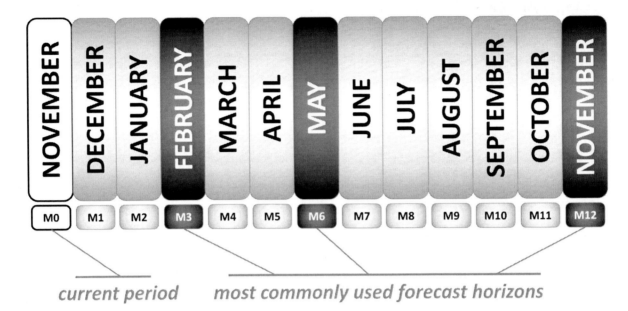

NOVEMBER	DECEMBER	JANUARY	FEBRUARY	MARCH	APRIL	MAY	JUNE	JULY	AUGUST	SEPTEMBER	OCTOBER	NOVEMBER
M0	M1	M2	M3	M4	M5	M6	M7	M8	M9	M10	M11	M12

current period   *most commonly used forecast horizons*

Figure 30 - Forecasting horizons

The illustrated example shows that the current month is November (yellow cell). The sales forecast for the current month is marked M0, a 3-month advance forecast (February) is M3, a 6-month advance (May) forecast is marked M6, and a 12-month advance forecast (another November) is marked M12.

There are organizations where operations are planned in weekly horizons and they require that forecasts be exact down to a week. If this is the case the logic behind marking forecast months should be *translated* to weekly forecast horizons (M12→W52, M6→W26) but a pragmatic approach which entails changing the nearest periods expressed in months into weeks, while the sales forecasts remain consistent with the operational planning.

As weekly horizons are usually dictated by the sales plans and in such case they are developed in two- or maximum three-month horizons, good practice is that translating the sales forecast into weeks refers to the basic horizon (M2 or M3) with a 2-3-week *'notice'*.

Then the forecast quality is measured in a normal way and the sales forecast in this time horizon (T9/T13) is easily *transferrable* for the purposes of operational planning of sales for all of its components (regular sales, promotions with set start and end dates, specific dates for introduction of the NPD).

Quantitative vs. Qualitative Forecast

There is one more important issue related to the forecasting process that needs to be accounted for at its implementation, namely the unambiguity of how it is expressed. Sometimes it is expressed as quantity and sometimes as value of the product. Having said that sometimes even the sales value of the product is unambiguous as there are various levels of the sales value (i.e. product sales, net sales, the I/II/III margin, etc.).

This issue stems from the fact that some divisions use the plans expressed with the value (Finance), while the other ones use the amount (Production, Logistics). The sales forces usually use the forecasts and plans which are expressed in values.

If the objective is to have a one forecast company then it is necessary to take this issue into account and create mechanisms which allow *to translate* value forecasts into quantity forecasts and vice versa.

The problem may seem banal as each product has its specific price and it should act as an easy converter between the sales quantity and value. So much for theory as the business reality is slightly more complicated.

First of all, the company may have organized the sales system based on various price lists assigned to a number of sales channels or even individual customers. In such case, the same sales volume achieves various sales values depending on the channel or the customer.

Even if there is one price list for all the customers at the company, the final prices for the customers may vary due to different trade terms which are negotiated and contracted on an individual basis. A simple solution then arrives, to prepare individually – for each customer – *'dictionaries'* that translate volume into value and vice versa. It is a solution but it becomes hard when the list of direct customers is long and may even include several thousand customers.

There is also another problematic issue which complicates direct translation of the sales volume into its value If the sales is not executed via a natural market demand but it requires promotional support, the final value of that support significantly impacts the end price for the customer. Moreover, it is important to remember that various promotional mechanisms (also in terms of value) may be applied across a number of

distribution channels (e.g. RETRO[13] discounts, BOGOF[14] promotions, etc.), which complicates direct conversion of the sales volume to value somewhat further.

Even though the issues pertaining to the price politics on the mass market of consumer goods is not easy there are solutions which allow to control it.

As the promotional activities are not executed by the sales forces at just any given time an within an unlimited budget (usually it is agreed in the customers' trade terms), the sales forecasts for specific terms are prepared by the sales managers or the sales control departments. Therefore, it is possible to plan and project which promotional activities will be performed via individual sales channels and when, with a rather high probability rate. It is then possible to estimate the costs of such support, and consequently, the final sales value in a given period. It takes place in case of every company so in order to quickly convert the sales volume to its value and back it is necessary just to organize communication between the persons responsible for preparation of such projections and the forecasting department's staff. It is clear that due to confidentiality of such information the team responsible for the sales forecasting should be authorized to gain access to it.

Successive acquisition and updating of such information is one part of the task, while the other part is to place it within some structure in the forecasting support systems, which should enable automatic conversion of the sales volume to its value and vice versa. Development of such systematic solution may not be an easy task but if it is done well and implemented it offers

---

[13] Retrospective discounts

[14] Buy One Get One Free promotion

immense benefits.

A solution of this issue shows what an important aspect is the intra organizational communication and cooperation, as well as the streamlining of information. After all it does confirm the thesis regarding qualifications of the sales forecasting team (refer to chapter *3. Sales Forecasting Team* page 43).

Sales Forecasting in relation to the organization key areas

As presented earlier, sales forecasting is in a way a natural axis for the processes which generate the company's added value and coordinate distribution of its products to end customer (i.e. the consumer of goods and services).

This process may also be viewed as the navigation center aimed at:

1. **Obtaining information** on the demand for the offered range of goods, its fluctuation over time (→ demand forecast) and on the resources necessary to meet that demand,

2. **Coordination of the flow of information** on availability of resources necessary to meet the demand (→ sales forecast).

The key areas which are affected by the sales forecasting process are presented hereunder in Figure 31 below.

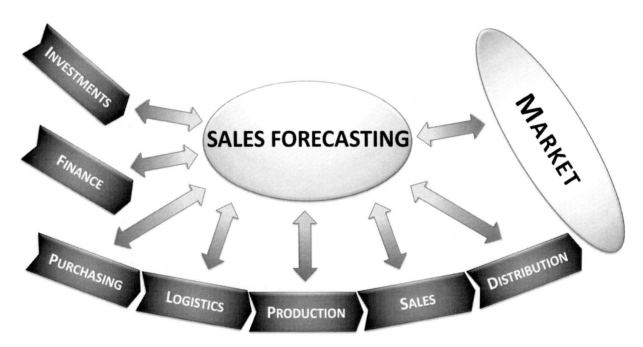

Figure 31 - Co-coordinating role of the forecasting process

Sales and Operations Planning

The first area of operations that comes to mind as related to forecasting of demand or sales is no doubt the **sales and operations planning**. The sales forecasting has been presented as separated from the sales planning on purpose since these are two different concepts as presented in one of the earlier chapters.

The sales plans are prepared based on the demand forecast. Although there may even be a situation where the sales plans affect the forecast, especially if the **sales plans** are to also include – apart from the actual sales plans – also the **promotional plans and marketing plans** in a broad sense.

Another stage after the sales plans have been generated is the appropriate planning of the ready goods' stock levels over time, and as a consequence preparation of the **production plans**:
- Proprietary production plans
- Sourcing plan

Once the production plans are developed, the next natural stage is the **planning of resources** that will allow to follow through on the planned production. Apart from **planning of materials, raw materials, components, unfinished products** etc., also the following are prepared at that stage:
- **production line performance** plans (including plans of changeovers, refurbishments, inspections, etc.),
- **employment** plans (seasonal or strategic plans for the HR development due to sales growth),

- **financial** plans (e.g. cashflow projections) if external financing is needed and for the purposes of necessary capital investment projects),
- **investment** plans – usually as a part of a strategic plan which includes investments in production lines, technology, knowhow, patents (and other broadly understood know-how), development of the logistics infrastructure (warehouses, transport), HR development (recruitment, training), etc.

It is clear that planning in all those areas is executed almost simultaneously. It is vital, however, to include the end results of the preceding plans in the consequent plans (in the order specified above). It is also the main role and at the same time a challenge for the forecasting team.

In the context of operational planning it is necessary to refer to the so called bullwhip effect. The bullwhip effect basically consists in reinforcement of the demand information and unwarranted increase of cyclical orders, while cascading them down to the next links in the supply chain from producer to consumer. This effect is shown hereunder, in the figure based on a simplified supply chain model presented on the Figure 32 below.

It is clear how in individual links of the supply chain the scale of orders increases. The main reasons for this phenomenon being:
- delays in order turnaround (t1, t2, t3, t4),
- using overly simple (naive) forecasting models in each link,
- forecasting for too short time horizons,
- limited communication or sharing of demand information in individual links of the chain.

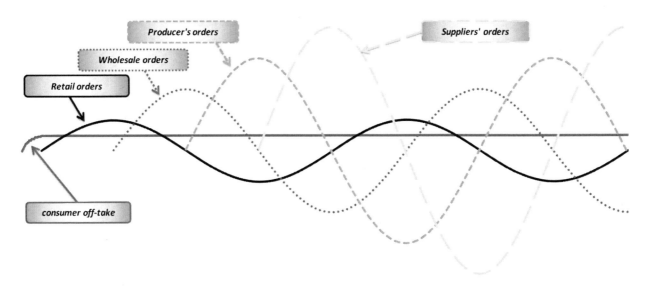

Retail orders

Wholesale orders

Producer's orders

Suppliers' orders

consumer off-take

Figure 32 - Bullwhip effect in the supply chain

It is a known fact that this is not financially beneficial in any link of the chain. When the quality of forecasts is low, there is a risk of generating unnecessary supplies which will either not be used or, in the best case scenario, will wait long for sales to the next link, while generating high stock carrying costs. This issue has been discussed in more detail in the chapter *Importance of Forecasting in Business* (page 14).

Product Life Cycle Management

Already the earlier chapters contained references to the product life cycle. This issue should be taken into account already at the process implementation stage but also at a later stage of the process management as it is inherent to the forecasting function. Although it is a domain of marketing, from the point of view of the person in charge of forecasting sales of products it is extremely important to know the stage of life of products offered as this determines forecasting methods to be applied so as to achieve better forecast quality. This does not necessary mean product management by the sales forecasting team, rather the ongoing and thorough exchange of information between the sales forecasting team and the marketing department or another department in charge of managing the product life cycle.

The PLC management concept adopts a certain model which describes the product life cycle. This concept refers to both the individual products and the entire product groups and categories, including brands.

This concept basically outlines 5 stages of the product life cycle:

1. Research & Development,
2. Introduction,
3. Growth,
4. Maturity,
5. Decline.

In the PLC management context, each of these stages implies different activities:

- **cashflow,**

- generated **profits**,
- adopted **marketing strategies**,
- **sales level and dynamics**, which in the forecasting context calls for use of

appropriately selected forecasting models. Fluctuations in the sales volumes and profitability at various stages of the product life cycle are illustrated in figure hereunder:

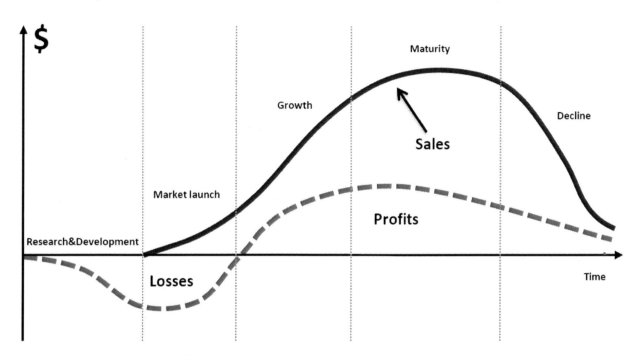

Figure 33 - Stages of product life cycle (sales and profitability)

1. **Research & Development** stage: from the point of view of sales forecasting and operational planning it is irrelevant. It is usually a tedious stage when a new product concept is developed, absorbing considerate capital outlays. The only element which is important from the point of view of sales planning is sales of the test products. Owing to the fact that only a marginal number of products prepared for market launching goes through to the next stage, at the forecasting stage it is only possible to develop long-term forecasts on a high level of product hierarchy; e.g. there will be product introduced in a specific category but it is not known yet which from many developed proposals.

2. **Market launch** stage is typically a

consequence of conducted research and the decision to market launch. It is usually low volume sales and its level depends on decisions of distributors who consider new products rather as a risk and are not keen on purchasing high volumes. It is the stage of selective distribution, rather limited. The must at this stage are close contacts with the sales forces which should submit on an ongoing basis the purchasing decisions of distributors. Another important element at this stage of product's life is that the products are usually supported very intensely by the sales and marketing campaigns. The selection of forecasting methods should take into account current trends and promotional sales.

3. **The growth** stage that follows is a result

of the product's acceptance by the market and sales showing a very strong growth trend. The sales and marketing support is decreased by then and if any, it is aimed not at awareness building but at distinguishing the product against the competition. It is possible at this moment to replace the product with its improved version or introduce new versions which expand the category. Prognostic methods should be selected in a manner that incorporates a strong growth and – if the product or category show such a trend – the seasonal sales element, and the promotional sales to a lesser extent. Close communication with the sales forces is required as – using the methods based on time series – the quickly increasing number of distributors and distribution channels for the new product may result in the sales level shift phenomenon.

4. **Maturity** stage is stabilization of sales on its maximum level. The product's recipient is mass consumer which clearly stabilizes the sales process, and this in turn allows to automate the statistical forecasting which most often is already without the trend element but here may still be the seasonal sales element. Still, if the product is classified in A category, then despite stability of the process the forecasts generated for that product should be regularly monitored and consulted with the sales forces which may be incentivized to bring in the promotional sales.

5. **The Decline** stage is the last period in the product's life during which, after a relatively long period of maximum and stable sales levels they begin to drop (the market is already satiated with the product). The product continues to be profitable but not to the same degree as before. Usually this is caused by promotions based on lowering the price so as to maintain the market shares (sales value is decreasing faster than the sales volume). The product is also successively withdrawn from the unprofitable distribution channels. In the forecasting context, methods used should account for the downtrend, the seasonal sales element, if any, and the infrequent promotional sales.

The standard product's life described above does not need to apply to all the categories a products. There are categories for which the cycles are different but nonetheless characteristic. Quoted hereunder are a few examples of such categories, including among others *Style*, *Fashion* or *Fad* i.e. *Seasonal Hit* (a temporary product craze/mania).

Furthermore, we are aware that the product life cycle today is becoming generally shorter and many products disappear from the market before they become generally recognized. Still, there are actions taken in order to prolong their market life as illustrated in Figure 36 below. Life extending actions include:

- change of the product's price,
- change of the promotional campaign (e.g. the marketing communication),
- improvement / restyling,
- transferring sales to a more efficient distribution channel,
- finding or creating new market segments,
- discovering new purposes for the product,
- repositioning the product, etc.

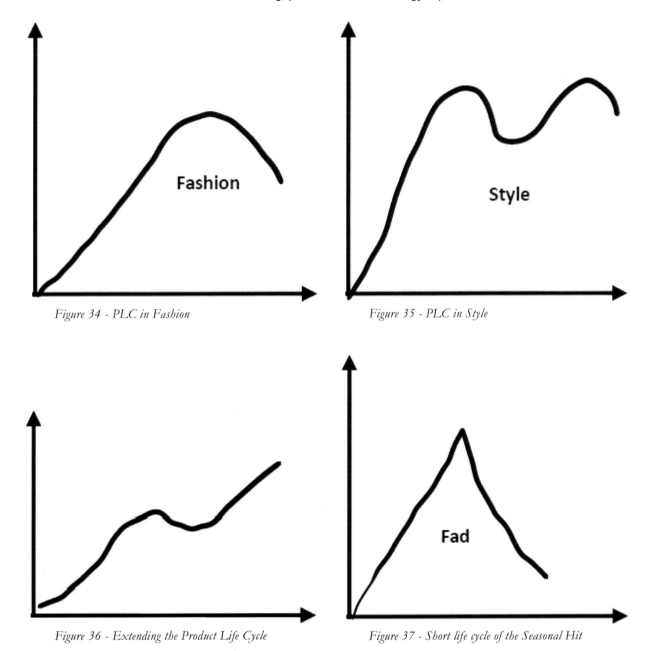

Figure 34 - PLC in Fashion

Figure 35 - PLC in Style

Figure 36 - Extending the Product Life Cycle

Figure 37 - Short life cycle of the Seasonal Hit

The PLC issues discussed above are very important in the context of the forecasting process and the methodology to be applied in order to significantly improve forecast quality. Thus, it is important to analyse product life cycles at least from time to time. The awareness of the product life cycle is also important in case of long-term forecasting which usually includes transitions between the individual stages of the product's life, and can even contain the entire life cycles (depending on the industry and the market). Guidelines related to such forecasts should be consulted with the departments which either introduced the products or are in charge of product management (i.e. Marketing, R&D).

It should be explicitly noted here that no company which reasonably manages its product portfolio allows for the situation where majority of the offered products is cumulated in the same stage of life rather than spread over various stages (apart from the Research & Development and Introduction stages which cover majority of products, which are then subject to market selection). This is conditioned by a long-term strategy whereby the mature products *'finance'* the products that at introduction and development stages. This renders forecasting methodology more comprehensive, which is something to be aware of.

Strategy Roll-Out and Strategic Management

Michael E. Porter writes that strategy boils down to acting differently than the competitors. He also underlines that the company may distance itself from the competition only if it can set itself apart and maintain it.

Contemporarily, one of the biggest challenges faced by organizations is management of the supply chain and establishing a competitive edge via optimization of that chain. After reading one of the earlier chapters we know that

In the book dedicated to implementation of strategy, entitled 'Implementation of strategy for achieving a competitive edge' , its authors, R.S. Kaplan and D.P. Norton, unanimously indicate how important an element of each strategy is the structural forecasting structure.

Presented hereunder is the strategy implementation plan, from the aforementioned book, where the forecasting process, together with its elements that are shared by the strategy implementation, have been clearly highlighted. Thus, it can assumed that the forecasting process is an indispensable element of every strategy and the elements referred to in the book, such as:

• meeting related to strategy review,
• key participants and order of those meetings,
• monitoring of forecast quality and review of operating plans,
• analysis of impact of forecasts on operating costs,
• financial projections,

are the same or the forecasting process management, referred to further on.

Apart from a clear impact of forecasting on the operating planning areas, any long-term forecasts, their monitoring and confronting them with medium- and short-term forecasts are key elements of strategy review and active management of the strategy.

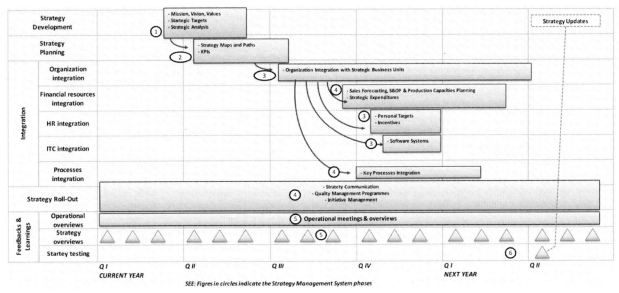

Figure 38 - Integrated strategy management process

Risk Management

Another element of every business that comes to mind in the context of forecasting are the risk management activities. Regardless of whether it is risk management in the context of projects or processes, the activities undertaken thereupon boil down to the following:

1. Risk management planning,
2. Risk identification,
3. Risk analysis,
4. Planning risk preventing activities,
5. Risk monitoring and control.

If the organization approaches risk management understood as monitoring and reducing the risk to the accepted level specified in the assumptions (usually stemming from the adopted and implemented strategy), then it is visible already at the first glance that two out of five items (2 and 5) are directly related to demand forecasting processes, sales and the related operational planning. As already noted in the introduction, it is not an intent of this publication to thoroughly analyse all the issues pertaining to forecasting but to identify them and their relation to the forecasting process.

I would like to refer everyone interested in risk management to the abundant literature on the subject. Across such literature we can certainly find the references to the sales forecasting. However, I am positive that based on the aforesaid and through analogy to the chapter on strategy, you are already aware of a close connection between the risk management process and the forecasting process, which needs to be taken into account upon its implementation.

Defining the Forecasting Cycle

In order to define and organize the so called forecasting cycle, it is important to first realize what this forecasting cycle is and what is the purpose of implementing it. If we remember the definition of the demand or sales forecast (chapter Basic Terms and Definitions, page 32), it should be noted that by definition it is set for specific market conditions. One must be aware that market conditions change one day to another (and sometimes even more frequently) and, in consequence, the sales forecasts change as often. Each piece of information about the market, new arrangements of the sales forces with the customers, each new agreed promotion, as well as any information about a change in output capacity of production lines, changes in fact the demand or the sales forecast.

Although the IT systems could perhaps keep up with such rate of changeability (on condition of consistent and immediate update of systems to include such information), the company's decision making processes involving the executive staff would not. Therefore, the so called **forecasting cycle** is defined, which enables work with the demand and sales forecasts in a pragmatic fashion (see definition above)

In one sentence, it is important to review the current forecast from time to time (perform and keep for some time the so called *snapshot of the forecast*) so that all the parties concerned can use this forecast for a specific period of time, as the only forecast in effect.

> **Forecasting Cycle** is a schedule of very specific activities which are repeated over fixed periods of time (usually on a monthly basis), performed at the company by dedicated units (individuals/teams) at a specific time, in order to:
>
> 1.**review** the results of the generated **sales** against the forecast and explain any variations,
>
> 2.**generate** and agree with all the process participants a new updated sales **forecast**,
>
> 3.**introduce** and agreed **forecast to the systems**, allowing for **further planning**, including the **operational** planning.

Participants and Stakeholders

The stakeholders of the forecasting cycle (process) are a group of individuals within the company, directly interested in its result, namely the current sales forecasts for the purposes of their individual tasks. Majority of these people are also the process **participants** who may perform the following functions as part of that process:

- supply information,
- process information (generate forecasts, analyses),
- coordinate process activities,
- make decisions,
- publicize and distribute the process results (effects).

By and large, the group **supplying** the information includes staff from all the departments involved, i.e. Sales, Marketing,

Production, Logistics, Purchases, Strategy, Finance, etc.

The group **processing** the information mainly includes the forecasting department, however, if processing refers to specific analyses (ABC, etc.) conducted at the company, other departments which conduct such analysis as a standard – as part of their function – should also be taken into account and actively used in the process (i.e. Marketing, Strategy, Finance, R&D, etc.).

The process **coordinating** role (sometimes referred to as the process owner) and responsibility for its correct functioning and delivering the results is usually assumed by the manager of the sales forecasting team.

Discretion for the **decision making** should in general lie with leaders of the departments involved, who make binding decisions regarding the demand and sales forecast. For instance, the heads of sales divisions usually have the decisive say when it comes to executing promotion in their divisions, product managers are responsible for introducing new products or supporting their sales, etc.).

A **decisive factor of key importance**, to be taken into account in the process, is the top management staff, often represented by the Management Board . In the forecasting cycle this level of decision making should be taken into account at the last stage of confirming the updated forecast or when ultimately resolving opinion differences due to which the ultimate forecast cannot be reached. Such situations may occur when:

- During the consensus meeting (defined in the next sections, entitled *Schedule*) no clear understanding is achieved with regard to the final forecast due to clearly conflicted guidelines and objectives of some departments of the company. In such case the meeting's result is the forecast which is agreed in some portion (e.g. the sales channel, the group of goods), and the minutes recording differences, listing the reasons for them. Such situations also occur when the representatives of the departments participating in meetings do not have the discretion make the decisions which define the ultimate forecast. In that case, based on the information obtained, such decision is taken by the Management Board, reaching a compromise at the top managerial level; such decision becomes effective.

- The generated sales forecast is significantly different than the adopted long-term sales plans, which, in consequence, threatens execution of the annual plan or other strategic objectives of the company. In such case the Management Board makes decisions aiming at bringing forecasts down to the adopted objectives, including the decisions on launching additional or reallocating current funding supporting the sales (promotional and marketing budgets, etc.). After taking such decisions, and therefore with new assumptions aimed at bringing the forecasts closer to strategic (annual) plans, the new forecasts are generated. The Management Board may not take such decisions, while accepting the existing discrepancies as justified and falling within the adopted strategy. It is unreasonable, however, to encourage the process leader to – put in simple terms – *'stretch'* the forecasts without taking decisions on the improvement steps, warranting such changes, as in such situation, the forecast manipulated in this way is, in fact, no longer a sales forecast.

Definitely, any decisions made at this level, as well as by any other decision making persons, should be conscientiously recorded in the minutes taken and, upon their authorization, published together with the final forecast.

Schedule

When it is already known who should be invited and involved in cooperation in the forecasting cycle, the schedule for this process may be defined. Such schedule typically includes the following steps:

1. Accounting for and **summarizing the actual sales** for the past period, consisting in:
   a. introducing to the forecasting support system the results of sales conducted in the past period (by sales unit, i.e. channel, region, customer base, group of goods, etc.),
   b. measurement of the resulting forecast errors, and
   c. explaining the reasons for such errors (discrepancies).
      In normal conditions, when the systems are correctly configured, obtaining information on the sales execution and measurement of the forecast errors are performed on the first business day of the following period, and finding the explanation should not take longer than another 2 business days.

2. Preparing the data and generating **demand forecasts**, using the **statistical methods** which include:
   a. *'clearing history'* of the past sales, based on collected information so that it is possible to apply objective methods,
   b. generating forecasts using statistical (objective) methods for the individual sales units.
      Depending on the level of intensity of promotional sales and the number of

difficult indices ($\rightarrow$Z class products) this stage should not take longer than 2 business days.

3. **Adding** to the obtained statistical sales forecast the regular elements of **promotional sales** and **NPD**, based on the functioning plan of promotional and marketing support and the plan for implementation of new products. It is important to be aware that aggregating the elements such as basic sale, promotional sale and NPD is more than just an arithmetic addition. It is a stage of intense communication with the departments in charge of promotional and marketing support and implementation of NPD, aiming at review of the aggregated sales forecast, including such factors as *'cannibalism'* of sales of promotional product versions on the standard product variants and the impact of introduction of NPD on the other offered products.

4. **Submitting** the initially developed forecasts to the parties concerned within the sales departments (mainly heads of the sales divisions and product managers) up for their opinion. A result of this stage is collecting all the comments and reservations to the submitted forecasts and other related recommendations and issues. This stage, together with the preceding one (adding elements of the forecast), should take up to 5 business days.

5. **Preparing a detailed forecast** based on feedback from the sales departments and **forwarding** it **to the operating departments** (i.e. Production, Logistics, Purchasing), in order to prepare their leaders to the 'Consensus Meeting' (defined hereunder). It must be noted that until this moment the achieved result is the demand forecast, i.e. the forecast

which reflects the alleged demand for products on the market. This stage should start and end within one business day and, together with the earlier stages, it is a preparation to another stage, crucial to the entire process.

6. **'Consensus Meeting'** is of key importance in the entire cycle. As its very name suggests, a result of this meeting is agreement on the final value of the updated forecast. The meeting is usually attended by heads of individual sales divisions, product managers, heads of operating departments and a representative of the finance function. During this meeting, its participants aim at achieving a compromise between a unanimous forecast and the situation and plans of the departments they represent (often their individual goals in the motivational systems). It is important to draw attention to the fact that at this stage the **demand forecast** is reviewed by the conditions of the operating departments and therefore it **becomes the sales forecast**, i.e. subject to how realistic the plans based on the demand forecast are, they either confirm its merits or, most often, downsize it to the level of available resources in the operating departments. Often during such meeting many conflicting issues occur as to which the parties cannot reach a compromise. A **result of the meeting** may then be the **discrepancies** that may occur from limitations of the operating departments, e.g.: production priorities favouring some product groups before others, limited availability of products for all the sales divisions, reaching a top threshold for the production costs, excluding after-hours work or work during statutory holidays. It is vital for the **discrepancies certificate** to list both their **causes** and **rationale** so

that the decision-making body (i.e. the Management Board), while trying to resolve a certain issue, be aware of all the conditions and know all the *PROs* and *CONs* arguments. If during a meeting a **consensus is reached** by all the parties participating, a result is the **updated forecast** proposal. It is very important for the meeting to be attended only by decision making authorities or – if *acting as* on their behalf, the persons authorized to take decisions on their behalf as it is **decision making meeting** and not a presentation meeting. It is also worth to note that not all the meeting's participants must attend simultaneously. Usually it is a rather time consuming event (4-8h) and it may be tedious for all the participants. Thus, it is worth to consider planning it so that the individual participants are present only when their attendance is necessary, i.e. to provide the required information, offer comment or make the necessary decisions. It is worth to repeat that previous stages are focused on preparing the participants to this meeting and during the actual meeting the meeting leader may require such preparation. And one more technical issue: with a complex sales and product structure and two-dimensional forecasts (value vs. quantity), it is necessary to use the system (or at least a spreadsheet) during the meeting, in order to enable among others:

a. presenting the forecast across a number of hierarchy levels and various sales aspects (region/sales channel, product group, etc.)
b. automatic recalculation of quantity-value units,
c. comparing forecasts to historical values,
d. recording forecast variants,
e. introducing notes to forecast variants,

explaining their corrections and entering notes to forecast variants, explaining their adjustments and reviews.

During the meeting, any opinions, reservations and comments should be recorded in the minutes of the meeting, especially including those concerning amendments introduced to the draft forecast, identifying the reason, author, date, etc. Such minutes should be distributed among the meeting participants by the end of the next business day after the meeting.

7. **Forecast presentation to the Management Board**: within 2-3 days after the 'Consensus Meeting' the process leader should present the result of the 'Consensus Meeting' to the company's Management Board. This is done in order to present the prepared forecast as a whole, indicate variations and their reasons. In case during the 'Consensus Meeting' no agreement is reached regarding the final shape[15] of the updated forecast, a certificate of variations and their reasons is drawn up, allowing the Management Board to resolve disputes and take final decisions. In case of an agreed forecast which largely varies from the annual sales plan, the Management Board may decide to launch or reallocate the promotional and marketing support in order to bring forecasts closer to the annual sales plan. Thus, during the meeting, it is necessary to use the reports which show:

a. split into the main product groups,
b. amendment of the forecast as compared to the previous version,
c. annual forecast (execution of sales up to the current period + forecast until the end of the year), as compared to the annual sales goal.

A result of such meeting are final decisions regarding the discrepancies and confirmation of the final forecast which following this meeting is provided to those concerned as final, together with recommended actions.

8. **Formal definition of the final sales forecast** and implementing it across the organization's information systems. Distribution of the finally agreed forecast for the purposes of operational planning and reporting systems. Such activities usually take no longer than one business day.

From this moment forward, the forecast becomes an officially confirmed piece of information, based on which the activities based thereupon may be taken, i.e. operational planning, financial projections, etc. From this moment of the cycle, when operational planning is executed, the sales forecasting team takes time to assess and develop forecasting methodology and process.

As it stems from the above, the key 'Consensus Meeting' should take place not later than mid of the following month (in case of a monthly cycle) so that the final decisions enabling operational planning are taken not later than the 20th of the following month. General outline of the entire cycle is illustrated in Figure 39 below.

---

[15] final forecast understood as not only its value but also the manner of its execution by individual sales divisions and product variants (regular vs. promotional)

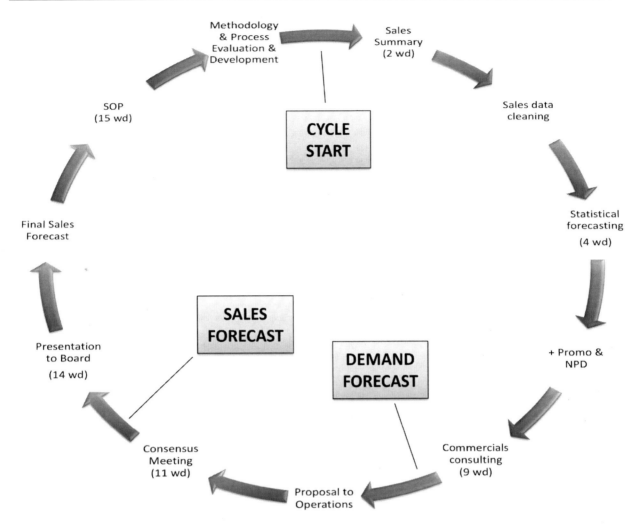

Figure 39 - General chart for a monthly forecasting cycle

Organization of Meetings

As it stems from the previously described schedule for the forecasting cycle, the process calls for at least two formal meetings planned over time: the 'Consensus Meeting' and the Presentation for the Management Board. Apart from those, there are ad-hoc meetings organized as part of the process whenever necessary.

It may happen that due to the organization's specifics or other conditions, Presentation to the Management Board is replaced by some other event which follows its objective. It may also turn out that regular meetings with e.g. marketing leaders or heads of sales channels will be necessary at an earlier stage of the cycle. However, regardless of these or similar modifications of the process, its fixed element MUST be the 'Consensus Meeting'.

Regardless of how many meetings and what type of meetings take place, and how many of them will be fixed and how many will be ad-hoc, all of them should be duly arranged and recorded. To that end:

- All the participants should be notified prior to each meeting of its date and place, best by email, also including the following information:
  - general agenda,
  - if the meeting does not require all the participants to be present simultaneously, a detailed schedule is necessary, specifying who should attend the meeting at what time ($\rightarrow$ this is not to take up time unnecessarily),
  - requirements for the participants, allowing them to prepare (e.g. collect to review the information necessary at the meeting),
  - if necessary, additional materials should be appended, allowing the initial review of specific issues,
  - request for confirmation of participation or nomination of the person to be present in case of absence, authorized to make decisions;
- during the meeting the person recording minutes (appointed before the meeting) makes note of the opinions of the participants on the items of the agenda discussed during the meeting, the issues raised, the proposals; in case of the 'Consensus Meeting' it should not be the process leader – their role is to moderate the meeting; a good practice is for the minutes to be taken by member of the forecasting team or employees of other departments, regularly attending such meetings – in such case the person recording the minutes should change by rotation during the following meetings;
- after each meeting the person recording the minutes creates a structured report on the meeting based on the prepared notes and sends it to the meeting's participants, which unanimously stating:
  - issues raised during the meeting,
  - decisions made,
  - proposals of other activities, who is responsible, when they should be completed and how they should be confirmed,
  - what side issues were raised, what follows from them, what proposals have been formulated and how should such information be dealt with (the person in charge, the deadline, etc.)

It is good practice to distribute the minutes of the meeting not later than EOB on the next business day after the meeting.

The meetings related to the forecasting process are specific in a sense that they require constant following of the main forecast and its elements. Hence, it is necessary during these meetings to have a constant access to the system supporting forecasting, that enables:

- following the forecast after introduction of changes, adjustments, reviews,
- creating new versions of forecasts and comparing one to another,
- submitting notes and comments regarding the introduced changes, etc.

It is recommended to use the available ICT technologies which can support the meetings, in case of dispersed organizational structure of the company. Organization of tele or video conferences with access to source materials (presentations, spreadsheets, etc.) proves very effective, especially in case of companies with international sales structure or when it is hard to get the decision making persons to meet in one place, as often as necessary. Nonetheless, even in case of applying advanced technologies to organize meetings as part of the forecasting cycle, it is always necessary to summarize them in the form of *'minutes'* of the meeting!

Process Communication

Majority of topics pertaining to the formal process related communication have been presented above. However, it is important to note that also the other communication channels require a similar approach with regard to preparation and summarizing. Every instance of communication related to exchange of information on the forecasting process (and not only that) should be documented, not necessarily in a standardized manner but an email summarizing the topics tackled and the decisions made is a correct way to go as it can always be used as reference to the topics discussed and decisions taken.

And this is not to create an expansive structure for information administration but to feel responsible for the taken decisions and respect time of others involved in the process. Acting this way facilitates everyday's work to a high degree and not only as part of the sales forecasting process. Here this aspect is stressed as the process related communication involves multidisciplinary teams to participate in a supra function process.

An important element of communication in the forecasting process is to build awareness among the process participants that any changes to the areas of their responsibility are important from the point of view of the process and should be immediately communicated to the sales forecasting team. That team, on the other hand, distributes the prepared information to the parties concerned.

This is to avoid generating surplus email correspondence mass sent across the company as *important* or *can be useful* or *just in case*. Many of us know the pain of piling through dozens or even hundreds of emails carbon copied to us but not really concerning us.

Reporting Results, Supporting System

One of the last issues that should be raised in relation to the forecasting process is reporting of the process results.

Considering such amount of data and information developed as part of the process, it is extremely important to focus attention on automation of its processing from the very beginning.

If the company works with several or several dozen indices, the spreadsheets, combined with office applications which enable publication of data on the intranet, will prove sufficient. However, if the company has a large portfolio of products, and an extensive structure of distribution channels, the idea of systemic process support is entirely justified.

There is a wide range of systems supporting the forecasting process on the market but not all of them can be scaled to fit the needs of every company, both in terms of financial solutions and the offered functions. Selection of such system is a very important decision and it should be duly prepared, thought through and justified.

It is vital to be aware that the system itself will neither solve problems nor support the organization in improvement of the sales forecasts. It is possible only with the people who deal with information affecting quality of forecasts. Therefore, the choice of system supporting the sales forecasting process is not a topic pondered by this publication and it is a secondary issue that becomes more obvious after the sales forecast becomes implemented by the company as an organizational process.

Let us then return to the issue of reporting. A dedicated system should be based on:

- standard database system connected with office applications used by the organization,
- IT services and technologies.

Why are such requirements posed? Because such system should ensure:

1. fast and automatic data updating (i.e. information on sales closed) obtained from the company's transactional systems (ERP, accounting),
2. review of such data based on the implemented logic and accuracy testing,
3. automatic calculation of the forecast quality indices ($\rightarrow$ forecast errors) in accordance with the adopted methodology,
4. automatic aggregation of forecasts an sales execution and forecast errors in any aspect (i.e. according to product hierarchy, distribution channel, etc.) in line with the adopted standard,
5. offering information in the form of reports (tables or charts) and in the form of numbers for further processing,
6. authorization and control of access to the publicized and offered information.

Such system should have a transparent structure comprehensible to all so that everyone concerned knows where to find the necessary information. Moreover, mobile user access has become a standard and it should be enabled also in case of such system.

The system of reporting and distributing the forecasting process results, organized in this manner, allows to avoid emailing information in the form of often large appendices to the process participants. Instead, it only sends notifications that the required information is available in the system.

Today every company has some database system or other so there is no need to invest in a system for the purposes of the forecasting process straight away.

It is important to be aware that this the system for storing and distributing the process results and the related information. It will not offer functionalities that enable generating automatic statistical forecasts or conduct analyses of the offered range of goods. Implementation of the system featuring such functionalities is, as already mentioned earlier, a serious decision, not necessarily taken at the stage of implementing the forecasting process, especially in case of small and medium companies.

SUMMARY

- Components of each sales forecast are the base sales, the promotional sales and the NPD; each of these components is subject to a different forecasting methodology.
- In order to optimize the forecasting process the offered range of goods should be appropriately grouped, while assigning characteristics obtained as a result of appropriately carried out analyses (i.e. ABC, XYZ).
- Prior to commencing forecasting it is necessary to appropriately select time series and the level of forecasting and to ensure the mechanism for recalculating the qualitative forecast over the quantitative one and back.
- The sales forecasting process is closely related to the company's key areas (i.e. Operations, PLC, Strategy), where the general guidelines should be obtained and the ongoing exchange of information, important from the forecasting process perspective, should be ensured.
- The sales forecasting process axis is the Forecasting Cycle whose key element is the so called 'Consensus Meeting'. In order to appropriately prepare it and launch it, the following elements must be considered and taken into account:
  - its participants and stakeholders,
  - schedule,
  - communication and meeting standards,
  - reporting and system support.

5. Forecasting Methodologies and Models

This chapter presents...
- how to effectively work with numerical data,
- description of selected models applied in sales forecasting based on time series:
  - fixed/stationary,
  - with trend,
  - seasonal,
  - seasonal with trend.

Who should read this chapter?

Before going any further, we should consider who this chapter is in fact dedicated to. It is too general for the specialists in the area of formal forecasting methods, while on the other hand it may seem too detailed for the managers who implement and manage processes, not necessarily interested in thorough statistical knowledge.

The intention of this chapter is to outline the basics of the objective forecasting methods in a comprehensible manner, regardless of the reader's statistical data competence, experience todate and function within the organization. The main purpose is to build a unanimous awareness and understanding of forecasting methods among all the forecasting process participants: both the managers and the formal (mathematical) methods' specialists.

It is recommended to take an approach whereby you either learn or revise the basics of the forecasting models and their application. This approach is mostly based on analysis of the presented sales forecast graphs and completing exercises using real sales data, using the formulas presented in the spreadsheets. Although presenting mathematical formulas for the individual models is unavoidable, they will not be the core of this chapter. These methods have been developed and are used by practitioners, aiming at various models of time series (i.e. various types of sales histories). They offer desired results only when they are appropriately selected and their parameters have been set accordingly.

Furthermore, it is important to be aware that each of the specified methods offers a different level of comprehensiveness. And here we arrive at one of the key forecasting issues, namely an appropriate **selection of method according to time series** as – according to one of the basic forecasting rules – there is no on universal method for all the model of sales 'behaviour'.

There are in fact statistical tests which enable method fitting to time series, nonetheless, this book focuses on expert assessment and manual selection in order to enable the reader to develop this precious competence. In practice, we are looking for the possibly most efficient method, while on the other hand we select the method which is possibly the simplest and optimal in the context:

1. calculation cost (time),
2. cost (time) of setting parameters,
3. understanding it by its users.

As already signaled at the beginning of this publication, the presented models do not exhaust the knowledge about the formal methods but still they are the basic ones, often used in business and generally they cover all the typical 'sales behaviours' of products.

In reference to one of the mentioned earlier forecasting rules, it is very important to use only the methods which are completely understandable by users. And generally this is the reason why this chapter has been written in such form and volume. It is aimed to help all those involved in the process understand the methodology.

The author believes that it is possible to select from the presented methods such methods which when appropriately set in terms in parameters and correctly understood will allow to significantly improve quality of sales forecasting at the company.

General Data Handling Rules

The purpose of this article is to revise the basic rules of working with data so as not to lose key information, important from the point of view of forming conclusions, on the one hand, while on the other hand using the data most 'ergonomically', in a way which is most natural for people, and to maintain objectivity of observation and conclusion.

First we should consider what facilitates the process of concluding so that it is both easier and faster. In other words: what does human mind (with some exceptions) favor: numbers or charts, and if charts which form is most successful?

Often data gets complied as in the following table (Figure 40):

Jan-07	Feb-07	Mar-07	Apr-07	May-07	Jun-07	Jul-07	Aug-07	Sep-07	Oct-07	Nov-07	Dec-07
51 455	38 003	52 127	45 403	43 557	54 132	39 981	48 440	45 662	51 875	39 605	50 515
Jan-08	Feb-08	Mar-08	Apr-08	May-08	Jun-08	Jul-08	Aug-08	Sep-08	Oct-08	Nov-08	Dec-08
45 770	40 266	47 151	53 987	46 486	44 802	47 358	51 317	59 607	42 407	34 297	50 375
Jan-09	Feb-09	Mar-09	Apr-09	May-09	Jun-09	Jul-09	Aug-09	Sep-09	Oct-09	Nov-09	Dec-09
54 317	46 095	46 160	49 494	40 427	46 370	54 610	40 443	46 671	40 361	41 134	36 106
Jan-10	Feb-10	Mar-10	Apr-10	May-10	Jun-10	Jul-10	Aug-10	Sep-10	Oct-10	Nov-10	Dec-10
44 725	43 343	59 722	46 817	43 907	49 028	47 091	34 465	42 265	58 371	47 719	43 886

Figure 40 - Simple comparison of a 4-year product sales history

We can then ask a question: how many of us can tell, at first glance, anything about that product's sales…? Another possibility to present the same data is hereunder:

Dane 1	January	February	March	April	May	June	July	August	September	October	November	December
2007	51 455	38 003	52 127	45 403	43 557	54 132	39 981	48 440	45 662	51 875	39 605	50 515
2008	45 770	40 266	47 151	53 987	46 486	44 802	47 358	51 317	59 607	42 407	34 297	50 375
2009	54 317	46 095	46 160	49 494	40 427	46 370	54 610	40 443	46 671	40 361	41 134	36 106
2010	44 725	43 343	59 722	46 817	43 907	49 028	47 091	34 465	42 265	58 371	47 719	43 886

Figure 41 - Comparison of sales histories which allows to compare corresponding periods

This comparison is already more user friendly as it at least allows users to quickly identify analogies across periods in individual years. However, how many analysts can conclude on that basis on the type and elements of the generated sales? Or, in fact, what are the differences in the sales structure in the next table? And, what's more, is it possible to forecast on that basis?

Dane 2	January	February	March	April	May	June	July	August	September	October	November	December
2007	16 635	20 273	3 208	10 296	15 825	31 739	52 025	25 065	19 675	5 156	6 130	7 149
2008	14 056	19 349	10 459	5 244	25 232	29 769	55 326	30 675	19 133	3 395	7 082	6 410
2009	17 831	23 001	6 956	7 227	23 997	28 166	48 267	26 749	24 061	7 388	8 045	5 500
2010	13 447	22 989	10 686	4 421	22 588	35 972	56 194	30 883	21 977	8 270	3 036	7 476

Figure 42 - Comparison of sales of another product

Perhaps the next two charts will be more self-explaining? They present the same data as the earlier tables. Both mark the historic sales trends with a blue line. (Note: here the solid line covers the grey line presenting the Actual Sales due to consistency of both series of data).

In addition, the charts show the Ex post forecast (here generated using the arithmetic mean formula), the forecast absolute error (AE) and the forecast absolute percentage error (APE).

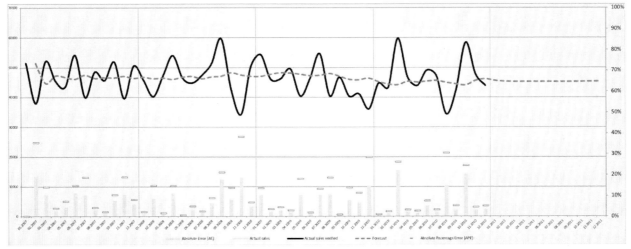

Figure 43 - Product 1 sales history chart together with Ex post forecast and errors

It is possible already at first glance to conclude the type of sales in both cases: the first one is the sales process at a specific level (stationary) with a lot of disruption (noise), and the other one is of course the seasonal sale.

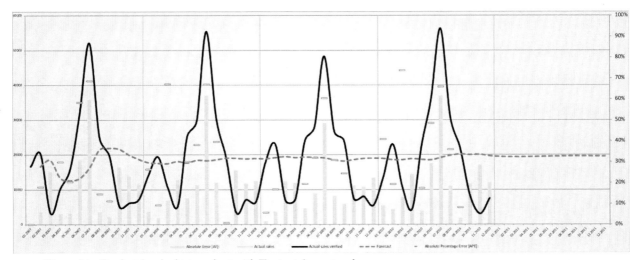

Figure 44 - Product 2 sales history chart with Ex-post forecast and errors

In case of charts – as in case of tables – it is vital to juxtapose on the chart the sales data in subsequent years – it is then easier to find the component which determines seasonality, if any– see Figure 45 hereunder.

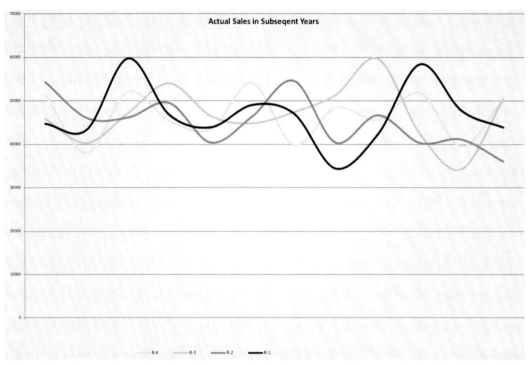

Figure 45 - Comparison of Product 2 sales in subsequent years

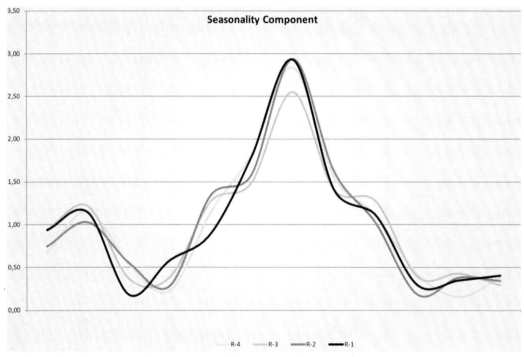

Figure 46 - Seasonality index chart for the following years of sale

It is easier still to find seasonality (not always identifiable in an ordinary visualization of history), when we can use the seasonality index chart – the Figure 46 above shows the chart related to data from the earlier table. To summarize this brief discussion of data presentation and concluding on that basis we should also refer to the scale of charts. Let us look over the two charts presented below in Figure 47 and Figure 48. They seem to be presenting two different sales histories, don't they? Let us note, however, the applied value scales...

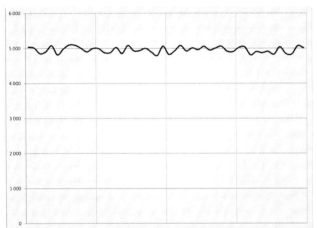

Figure 47 - The first of two 'different' sales history charts

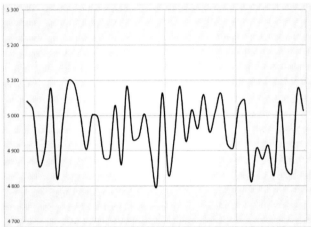

Figure 48 - The second of two 'different' sale history charts

It is one and the same sales process but show in different scales. Seems banal but in situations of taking important decision such elements of being *under the impression* unfortunately influence quality of such decisions.

Many times it can be observed in organizations that they either use this data presenting element in an unskilled or 'too skilled' way, which in many instances may be seen as proof of manipulation.

SUMMARY
- Data analysis in charts is much more effective for a human mind and more intuitive than analysis of data in tables – it enables quick identification of factors which influence sales, adjustment of history for the purposes of statistical data, selection of appropriate time for forecasting and identification of structural breaks in the time series model.
- Basic sales history flows must be visualized on time charts with even time intervals.
- Additional charts should be used, allowing to identify disruptions an elements of the sales level, trend, seasonality.
- The same chart proportions and similar value scales should be used (best if minimum always equals 0) and inbuilt trend functions should be used, allowing to identify the levels (*steepness*) of trends and time distance always in the same way.
- The same types of lines and colour codes should always be used (bright colours such as red, orange, yellow, are usually used to mark errors, irregularities, alerts).

Model description system

Before we move on to discuss individual methods, it is important to get to know the system used in mathematic description of models for ease of moving models to tools and systems used by the organization:

- **A** : actual sales value – realized, recorded,
- **F** : forecast,
- **e = A – F** : error made in sales forecasting,
- **t** : specific period of time (t or t_0 – current period),
- **h** : forecasting horizon,
- $\mathbf{F_{t+h|t}}$: forecast developed over a period t for a period t+h (or in simplification F_{t+h} as by default forecast is developed in period t),
- $\mathbf{A_t}$: actual sales value over a period t,
- $\mathbf{e_{t|t}}$: forecast error over a period t calculated over a period t (or in simplification e_t as by default these calculations are conducted immediately after the sales period ends),

- $\mathbf{L_t, T_t, S_t}$ – forecast components that stand for, respectively, the forecast sales level, trend and seasonality over a period t (for the models based on the exponential smoothing),
- **α, β, γ** : parameters (alpha, beta, gamma) for the forecasting models based on the exponential smoothing,
- **φ** : damping coefficient for the models containing damping coefficient.

Examples of formal description of values related to forecasting are presented in the following table (Figure 49).

The presented description standard is a universal one and gets widely used in the sales forecasting area but nonetheless it is important to be aware that literature on the subject may suggest other ways of describing the models and phenomena presented further.

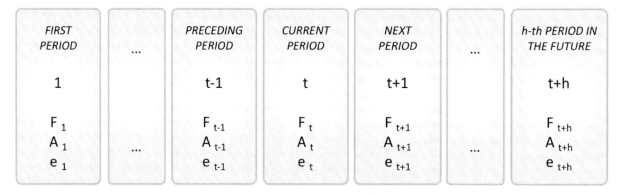

FIRST PERIOD	...	PRECEDING PERIOD	CURRENT PERIOD	NEXT PERIOD	...	h-th PERIOD IN THE FUTURE
1		t-1	t	t+1		t+h
F_1		F_{t-1}	F_t	F_{t+1}		F_{t+h}
A_1	...	A_{t-1}	A_t	A_{t+1}	...	A_{t+h}
e_1		e_{t-1}	e_t	e_{t+1}		e_{t+h}

Figure 49 - Examples of formal descriptions of values related to forecasting

Introduction to forecasting based on time series

Methods based on analysis of time series are the ones which based on historic data can identify the past behaviour model and on that basis they are able to predict future values.

The collected material describes the methods which are applicable upon specific models of behaviour, such as:

- **fixed level** – such time series are described as fixed and have a value in each period but do not show any trend or seasonality, in other words, subject to a big or small error they keep a certain fixed level of sales; they should not include the intermittent model, where for majority of time periods in question, no sales are generated;
- **trend** – time series in the past, showing from period to period either increasing or decreasing sales (uptrend or downtrend);
- **seasonality** – time series which in certain cycles (usually annual) show repetitiveness of behaviour and do not keep a fixed level of sales over the entire cycle period; it is rather clear that in order to use the methods for seasonal sale the sales history for at least one whole sales season (usually one year) must be readily available;
- **combinations** of the above.

When reviewing the main statistical forecasting methods for time series, we must stress that the presented ones are the most basic. Still, they are presented in such a way that the reader, not dealing with the statistical or mathematic use on an everyday basis, can on the one hand understand how they work, while on the other take individual decisions to apply them.

For educational purposes, the methods for regular time series have been reviewed in the following order:

- for stationary series:
  - o 1st Type Naive,
  - o Arithmetic Mean,
  - o Moving Average,
  - o Weighted Moving Average,
  - o Brown's exponential smoothing,
- for time series with trend:
  - o 2nd Type Naive,
  - o Arithmetic Average for the Trend,
  - o Moving Average for the Trend,
  - o Weighted Moving Average for the Trend,
  - o Holt's Exponential Smoothing,
  - o Gardner's Exponential Smoothing,
- for series showing seasonality:
  - o 3rd Type Naive,
  - o Winters' Exponential Smoothing,
- for series showing seasonality and trend:
  - o Holt-Winters Exponential Smoothing.

Models for stationary time series

The models dedicated to stationary time series imply that in each future period the sales will remain at a certain level, set in an appropriate way (subject to adopted model) based on historical sales data accepted for analysis. These models do not take into account any trends or seasonality or sales disruptions.

1st Type Naive Model

The 1st Type Naive Model assumes that the forecasting value equals the last observation value. This is shown in the Figure 50 below.

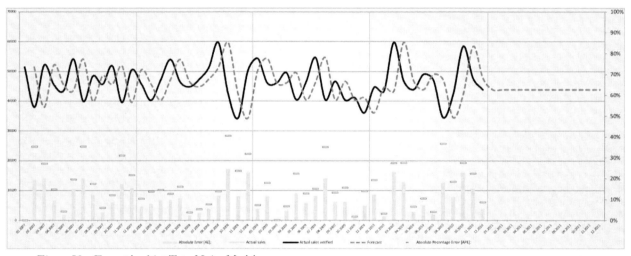

Figure 50 - Example of 1st Type Naive Model

This method is formally noted with the following formula:

$$F_{(t+1|t)} = A_t$$

where:

forecast F *for another period (t+1) is developed in the current period t and equals the sales value A, observed (generated) in the current period t.*

As clearly noticeable then, the forecast (green line) for the future and subsequent periods is the value of the last sales result. It is the simplest forecasting method which does not meet the basic expectation which is to 'filter out the disruptions' from the structure (here: the level) of sales. It rarely proves effective in business applications and if it does it requires very stable sales. More often used as benchmark for other methods.

In the spreadsheet it is necessary to test the historical sales data showing various flows (fixed, showing a trend or seasonality, incontinuous) and to calculate any error of such forecast (refer to the next chapter Measurement of Forecasting Quality). Conclusions regarding the possibilities and limitations of such method and possibilities of its practical application easily come to mind.

Arithmetic Mean Method

The arithmetic mean method assumes that the forecast value will equal the arithmetic mean of all the available observations, thanks to which it is possible to filter out the disruptions to a high extent. The principle of this method is outlined in the following formula:

$$F_{t+h|t} = \bar{A} = \frac{1}{t}\sum_{i=1}^{t} A_i$$

where if we assume that we are interested in the forecast for the next period (h=1) the formula is as follows:

$$F_{t+1|t} = \bar{A} = \frac{1}{t}\sum_{i=1}^{t} A_i$$

where:

forecast F *for the next period (t+1) developed in the current period t equals the arithmetic mean of all the observed (generated), available from the beginning (t=1) sales results Ai, up to the current period inclusive.*

Namely, the forecast adopted for subsequent periods is the arithmetic mean of all the observed sales results.

EXAMPLE OF HOW IT WORKS:

Forecast according to this model (dotted line on the chart) for the same set of data as in case of naive method, is shown in Figure 51 below. Already at the first glance, it is noticeable that the level of error (cream bars) is noticeably lower.

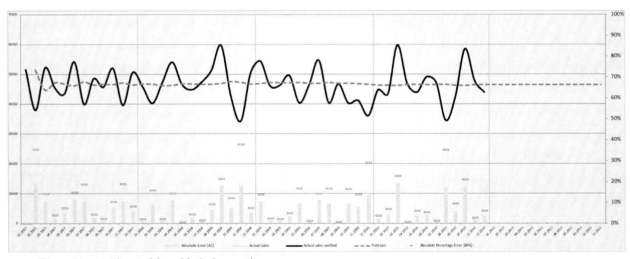

Figure 51 - Arithmetic Mean Method example

Implementation in the spreadsheet, in the simplest form, may be as follows:

	A	B	C	D	E	F	G	H	I
2			t :	1	2	3	4	5	6
3	INPUT DATA		Year :	2007	2007	2007	2007	2007	2007
4			Month :	1	2	3	4	5	6
5			Date :	Jan-07	Feb-07	Mar-07	Apr-07	May-07	Jun-07
6			Actual Sales :	51455	38003	52127	45403	43557	54132
8			Actual Sales Verified :	51455	38003	52127	45403	43557	54132
10			Forecast :		51455	44729	47195	46747	=AVERAGE($D8:H8)

Figure 52 - Example of implementation of the Arithmetic Mean Method

ISSUES RELATED TO THE MODEL:
- this model does not offer any parameters allowing to control the model and quality of forecasts,
- every result noted in the past carries the same weight when calculating the average, and therefore
- all the observations from the beginning equally influence the end forecast,
- all the *anomalous* observations also have the same weight and influence the forecast - problems occur when in the past there were interruptions, impulses or significant changes in the level of sales.

Moving Average Method

The moving average method is a method which includes a specific number (k) of the last observed sales results and the principle of that method is outlined in the following formula:

$$F_{t+h|t} = \frac{1}{k} \sum_{i=t-k+1}^{t} A_i$$

where:

forecast F *for another period (t+h, where h=1) developed in the current period t equals the arithmetic average for the last k observed/obtained Ai sales results, inclusive of any current sales.*

In other words the forecast for subsequent periods is the arithmetic mean of k from the recently recorded sales results.

A parameter in this model is the number of k periods, used to calculate the average and this number specifies the smoothing strength (→the more k periods the higher the smoothing strength), nonetheless both the closer and further periods from the time perspective have the same importance when it comes to setting the forecast for future periods. It eliminates the 'noise' which causes variability of results, thus offering the forecast structure.

EXAMPLE OF HOW IT WORKS:

The forecast chart for the same set of data as for the naive method, for a 6-month moving average, is presented hereunder:

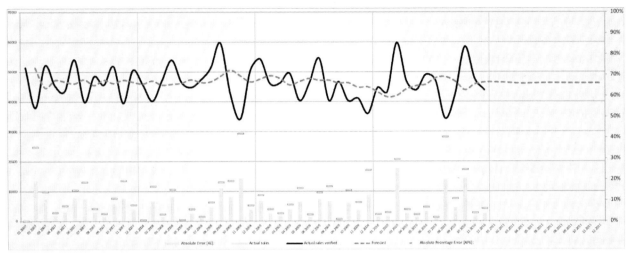

Figure 53 - Example of application of the 6-month Moving Average Method

It clearly shows that quality of forecast is also significantly higher when compared to the naive method.

SPREADSHEET IMPLEMENTATION EXAMPLE:

Implementation of this method in the spreadsheet k=6 may be as follows:

	A	B	C	D	E	F	G	H	I	J	K	L
2			t :	1	2	3	4	5	6	7	8	9
3		INPUT DATA	Year :	2007	2007	2007	2007	2007	2007	2007	2007	2007
4			Month :	1	2	3	4	5	6	7	8	9
5			Date :	Jan-07	Feb-07	Mar-07	Apr-07	May-07	Jun-07	Jul-07	Aug-07	Sep-07
6			Actual Sales :	51455	38003	52127	45403	43557	54132	39981	48440	45662
8			Actual Sales Verified :	51455	38003	52127	45403	43557	54132	39981	48440	45662
10			Forecast :		51455	44729	47195	46747	46109	47446,2	45533,8	=AVERAGE(F8:K8)

Figure 54 - Exemplary implementation of the 6-month Moving Average Method

ISSUES RELATED TO APPLICATION OF THIS METHOD:
- specification of the optimal length of the 'smoothing period' average, namely the k parameter,
- all the considered Ai results have the same impact on the value of the average, i.e. the forecast (they obtain the same 1/k weights).

As a result of the above the following problems occur:
- the problem of structural interruptions in the time series causes undesired forecast disruptions,
- the problem of outliers occurring in a time series causes similar forecast disruptions,
- temporary changes of the sales level in the observed time series also causes a big problem.

Weighted Moving Average Method

A certain improvement of the Moving Average Method is the Weighted Moving Average where the weight of the observed results included to calculate the average are fundamentally different and set as model parameters. The principle which this method is based on is prescribed by the following formula:

$$F_{t+h|t} = \sum_{i=t-k+1}^{t} (\omega_i \cdot A_i)$$

where:
- *the weight of individual observation A_i is given by ω_i,*

- *the weight of all the included observations ω_i give a sum total of: $\sum \omega_i = 1$,*
- *the order of weights in the average is given by k.*

EXAMPLE OF APPLICATION:

An example of this model for k=4 and weights ω, respectively 0.15, 0.25, 0.25, 0.35 is shown in Figure 55 hereunder. Quality of forecasts is significantly improved as compared to the naive method, and comparable to the earlier described average methods.

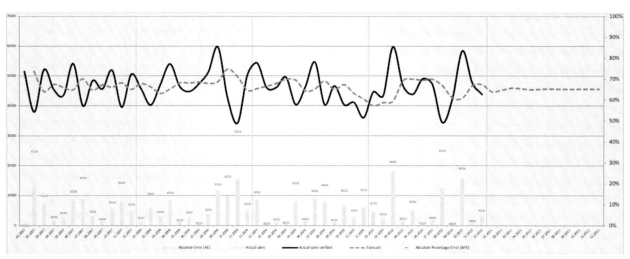

Figure 55 - Exemplary application of the Weighted Moving Average Method

However, it is clear that the factor where the forecast follows the most recent sales results Ai is clearly reinforced. Let's remember, however, that the comparison is performed on the same set of historical data. The effects could vary for historical data showing a different sales structure.

SPREADSHEET IMPLEMENTATION EXAMPLE:

An example of implementation of this method in the spreadsheet for historical data as in previous data and with the parameters set above (k=4 and ω weights respectively 0.15, 0.25, 0.25, 0.35) is shown below:

	A	B	C	D	E	F	G	H	I
3			Year :	2007	2007	2007	2007	2007	2007
4			Month :	1	2	3	4	5	6
5			Date :	Jan-07	Feb-07	Mar-07	Apr-07	May-07	Jun-07
6			Actual Sales :	51455	38003	52127	45403	43557	54132
8			Actual Sales Verified :	51455	38003	52127	45403	43557	54132
10			Forecast :		51455	44729	47195	46141,8	=SUM(E8*$B$11;F8*$B$12; G8*$B$13; H8*$B$14)
11		0,150							
12		0,250							
13		0,250							
14		0,350							

Figure 56 - Exemplary implementation of the 4-month Weighted Moving Average

ISSUES RELATED TO APPLICATION OF THIS METHOD:

The main issues related to using this method include:

- specification of the optimal length of the 'smoothing period' of the average (k),
- the observed results have a varied impact on the moving average, i.e. the forecast, but the appropriate selection of their weights ω requires good knowledge of the nature of the ales phenomenon,
- when there is a long smoothing period for each observed period it is necessary to set an appropriate weight, which causes complexity of calculation formulas and increases complexity of calculations.

Despite certain advancement and significant level of calculation complexity, this method still poses problems, mainly related to selection of weight parameters for individual observations, which requires a very good knowledge of nature of the sales phenomenon and still does not allow for a complete elimination of problems related to:

- structural breaks in time series,
- outliers which occur in the historical data sets,
- temporary change in the sales level in the observed time series.

Brown Single Exponential Smoothing

Brown's Single Exponential Smoothing Method is a method which is a development on the Weighted Moving Average, as its model assumes that the weights for individual observations affecting the forecast must vary but it also:

- pays more attention to observations closer in time,
- decreases the weight equally to the observations becoming further down in the past,
- assumes an exponentially weighted moving average.

This idea is presented in the following formulas (here the weights are replaced with ω symbol):

$$F_7 = \underset{\omega}{0.5 \cdot A_6} + \underset{\omega \cdot \omega}{0.25 \cdot A_5} + \underset{\omega \cdot \omega \cdot \omega}{0.125 \cdot A_4} + \underset{\omega \cdot \omega \cdot \omega \cdot \omega}{0.0625 \cdot A_3} + ...$$
$$for : \omega = 0.5$$

and exponential smoothing is obtained by a respective exponential reduction of weight:

$$\alpha_0 = (1 - \alpha)^0 \cdot \alpha = \alpha$$

$$\alpha_1 = (1 - \alpha)^1 \cdot \alpha = (1 - \alpha) \cdot \alpha$$

$$\alpha_2 = (1 - \alpha)^2 \cdot \alpha$$

$$\alpha_3 = (1 - \alpha)^3 \cdot \alpha$$

...

Using the function's recurrence and combination of 2 of the following ideas, whereby:

- the weight of future observations in a time series, namely their importance to the forecast, must decrease as *the age* of those observations increase - the most recent values of observations are more important than the older ones,
- the forecast error that occurs in the current period et should be included in the next calculated forecasts - past forecast errors should be taken into account for the next and any subsequent forecast,

the **Simple Exponential Smoothing**

Method, also referred to as the **Linear Exponential Smoothing** or **Brown's Exponential Smoothing** (after its author's name) has been developed.

The formal notation of this method can be found in the following equal formulas:

$$F_{t+1} = \alpha \cdot A_t + (1 - \alpha) \cdot F_t$$

$$F_{t+1} = F_t + \alpha \cdot e_t$$

where:

F_{t+1} – *forecast sales value over the next period (after the current one) t+1,*

α – *alpha smoothing parameter (where $0 \le a \le 1$),*

F_t – *value of sales forecast calculated for the current period t,*

A_t – *value of sales earned/observed for the current period,*

e_t – *forecast error margin in the current period t.*

It must be noted that selection of the damping factor α, which is a parameter for this method, is very important.

Exponential value decrease for individual observations in the past

t \ α	0,0	0,1	0,2	0,3	0,4	0,5	0,6	0,7	0,8	0,9	1,0
t	0,0000	0,1000	0,2000	0,3000	0,4000	0,5000	0,6000	0,7000	0,8000	0,9000	1,0000
t-1	0,0000	0,0900	0,1600	0,2100	0,2400	0,2500	0,2400	0,2100	0,1600	0,0900	0,0000
t-2	0,0000	0,0810	0,1280	0,1470	0,1440	0,1250	0,0960	0,0630	0,0320	0,0090	0,0000
t-3	0,0000	0,0729	0,1024	0,1029	0,0864	0,0625	0,0384	0,0189	0,0064	0,0009	0,0000
t-4	0,0000	0,0656	0,0819	0,0720	0,0518	0,0313	0,0154	0,0057	0,0013	0,0001	0,0000
t-5	0,0000	0,0590	0,0655	0,0504	0,0311	0,0156	0,0061	0,0017	0,0003	0,0000	0,0000
t-6	0,0000	0,0531	0,0524	0,0353	0,0187	0,0078	0,0025	0,0005	0,0001	0,0000	0,0000
t-7	0,0000	0,0478	0,0419	0,0247	0,0112	0,0039	0,0010	0,0002	0,0000	0,0000	0,0000
t-8	0,0000	0,0430	0,0336	0,0173	0,0067	0,0020	0,0004	0,0000	0,0000	0,0000	0,0000
...											
∞	1,0000										

values whose weight is at least 5% of the total weight

As it stems from the table above, with the parameter α = 0.1 almost the entire weight (95%) of observations included in the forecast for another period is distributed over 8 most recent sales observations in the past. For α = 1 the model adopts a form of a naive method.

Based on empirical experience the following guidelines may be used when selecting the α factor:

- α factor should fall within the range from 0.1 to 0.5 (maximum),

- the higher the fluctuations in the observed values in the past, the lower should be the value of α factor,
- if relatively lower forecast error values are obtained for α > 0.5, it may mean a mismatched forecasting model.

EXAMPLE OF APPLICATION

Below is a chart presenting the forecast obtained using the exponential smoothing method for α = 0.114:

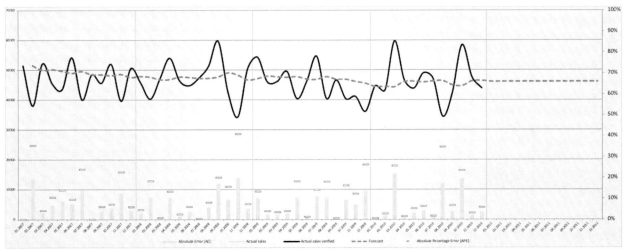

Figure 57 - Example of the Exponential Smoothing Method for a = 0.114

SPREADSHEET IMPLEMENTATION EXAMPLE:

An example of implementation in the spreadsheet may look as presented below:

	A	B	C	D	E	F	G
2			t :	1	2	3	4
3	INPUT DATA		Year :	2007	2007	2007	2007
4			Month :	1	2	3	4
5			Date :	Jan-07	Feb-07	Mar-07	Apr-07
6			Actual Sales :	51 455	38 003	52 127	45 403
8			Actual Sales Verified :	51 455	38 003	52 127	45 403
10			Forecast :		51 455	49 921	=$B$11*F8+(1-
11		0,114					$B$11)*F10

Figure 58 - Example of implementation of Brown's Exponential Smoothing Method

113

ISSUES RELATED TO APPLICATION OF THIS METHOD

Limitations of the Simple Exponential Smoothing method:

- the main limitation of this method, as in case of those referred to earlier, is exclusion of any trend, which results in a situation where from a certain moment in the future forward the forecasts for future periods form a straight horizontal line,

- therefore, this method is not always suitable for forecasting products showing a trend as by assumption it will be delayed comparing to any trend.

Models for time series featuring a trend

Time series showing a trend are those which in the observed periods in the past, from period to period show either growing or dwindling sales (namely the up or down trend sales).

The basic methods referred to in this publication are consistent with the stationary time series but still they allow to successfully forecast time series featuring a trend.

The 2nd Type Naive Method

The Naive Method is the simplest forecasting method for trend showing series. It assumes that further sales growths (or decline) in the following forecast periods will be the same as the sales growth (decline) for the current period. In general, it takes into account solely the (up or down) trend from the most recent observation period to calculate forecasts for future periods.

The mathematical representation of this method is in the following formula:

$$F_{t+h|t} = A_t + h \cdot (A_t - A_{t-1})$$

where:

F forecast *for future periods (t+h, where h denominates a multiple of the forecast horizon, usually = 1) developed in the current period t, equals:*

A_t – *the sales value observed in the current period t, plus (or minus) the difference between the sales levels in the current and the most recent period $(A_t\text{-}A_{t-1})$ times, respectively, a multiple of the h forecast horizon.*

The principle underlying this method is illustrated by Figure 59 below.

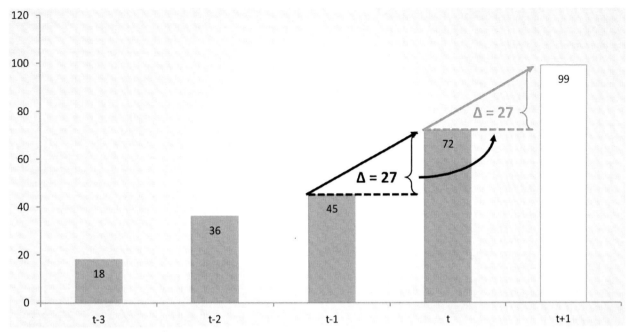

Figure 59 - Principle of the 2nd Naive Method

EXAMPLE OF APPLICATION

The chart below shows an example of the forecast obtained using this method for the data that shows a downtrend:

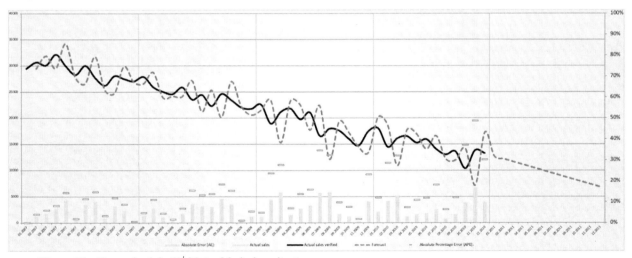

Figure 60 - Example of the 2nd Naive Method application

SPREADSHEET IMPLEMENTATION EXAMPLE

This method is presented in the spreadsheet here below:

	A	B	C	D	E	F	G	H
2			t :	1	2	3	4	5
3			Year :	2007	2007	2007	2007	2007
4		INPUT DATA	Month :	1	2	3	4	5
5			Date :	Jan-07	Feb-07	Mar-07	Apr-07	May-07
6			Actual Sales :	29 428	30 629	30 054	32 112	29 905
8			Actual Sales Verified :	29 428	30 629	30 054	32 112	29 905
10			Forecast :		29 428	31 830	29 479	=G8+(G8-F8)

Figure 61 - Example of implementation of the 2nd Naive Method in spreadsheet

ISSUES RELATED TO APPLICATION OF THIS METHOD

The method's biggest limitation is that the basis for calculation of further forecasts is only the last observed trend, which may be confusing for instance in situations when after a long-term sales growth there is a sudden 1-period long collapse and decrease in sales. Then any further forecasts based on such situation may prove very costly to the company and cause OOS (out of stock) situations.

Arithmetic Average Method with the Trend

Correspondingly to the stationary series, a natural improvement of the 2nd Naive Method is averaging all the observed growths (trend ratios) and calculating forecasts for the subsequent periods thereupon.

A formal, mathematic notation of this method is provided by the following formulas:

$$F_{t+h|t} = A_t + h \cdot \bar{\Delta}$$

where:

$$\bar{\Delta} = \frac{1}{(t-1)} \sum_{i=2}^{t} (A_i - A_{i-1})$$

and

F – *forecast for the subsequent periods (t+h, h being a multiple of the forecast horizon, usually = 1), developed in the current period (t),*

A_t – *sales value observed over a given period (t),*

Δ – *average of all the observed differences in the sales levels,*

h – *forecast horizon (number of the forecast period in the future).*

The principle of application of this method is illustrated hereunder:

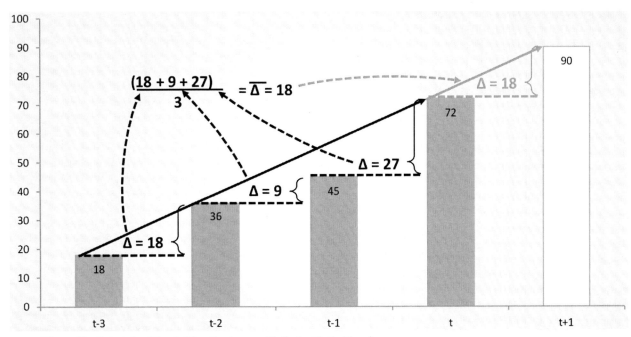

Figure 62 - Principle of the Arithmetic Average Method with the Trend

EXAMPLE OF APPLICATION

This chart shows how this method works with a trend:

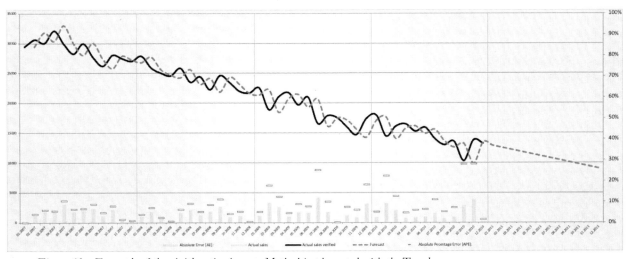

Figure 63 - Example of the Arithmetic Average Method implemented with the Trend

SPREADSHEET IMPLEMENTATION EXAMPLE

An example of implementation of this method in the spreadsheet is presented hereunder:

	A	B	C	D	E	F	G	H	I
2			t :	1	2	3	4	5	6
3			Year :	2007	2007	2007	2007	2007	2007
4	INPUT DATA		Month :	1	2	3	4	5	6
5			Date :	Jan-07	Feb-07	Mar-07	Apr-07	May-07	Jun-07
6			Actual Sales :	29 428	30 629	30 054	32 112	29 905	28 240
8			Actual Sales Verified :	29 428	30 629	30 054	32 112	29 905	28 240
10			Forecast :		29 428	31 830	30 367	33 007	=H8+AVERAGE(
11	Forecasting	0,000							$E14:H14)
12		0,000							
13		0,000							
14		0,000	Delta :		1 201	-575	2 058	-2 207	-1 665

Figure 64 - Implementation of the Arithmetic Average Method with the Trend

ISSUES RELATED TO APPLICATION OF THIS METHOD

Thanks to this method the forecast trend is well averaged and the method works rather well with an evenly increasing (or decreasing) sales, however, it loses its impact in situations when the trend clearly changes in the last observed periods or it breaks and changes direction to the opposite (e.g. covering several periods, a regular drop following a long-term growth). In such situations one of the following methods presented in this section is more appropriate.

Moving Average Method used with the Trend

Correspondingly to the method for the stationary series, this method also takes into account only a specific number of the recently observed growths (downs) which it accounts for when calculating sales forecasts for the subsequent periods.

Formally, it is presented by the following formulas:

$$F_{t+h|t} = A_t + h \cdot \bar{\Delta}$$

where:

$$\bar{\Delta} = \frac{1}{k} \sum_{i=t-k+1}^{t} (A_i - A_{i-1})$$

and

F – *forecast for the subsequent periods (t+h, where h is a multiple of the forecast horizon, usually = 1) calculated in the current period (t),*

A$_t$ – *sales value observed in a given period (t),*

Δ – *average of the observed differences in the sales levels in the recent periods (k),*

h – *forecast horizon (number of the forecast period in the future),*

k – *number of the recent observations (sales results) taken into account when calculating the average (i.e. forecast).*

The principle of this method is illustrated hereunder:

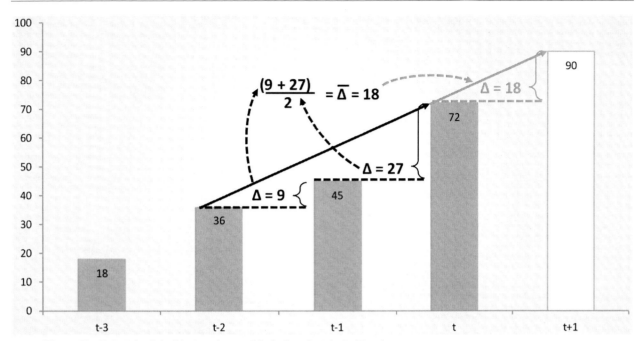

Figure 65 - Principle of the Moving Average Method used with the Trend

EXAMPLE OF APPLICATION

Presented below is how the method works with the trend:

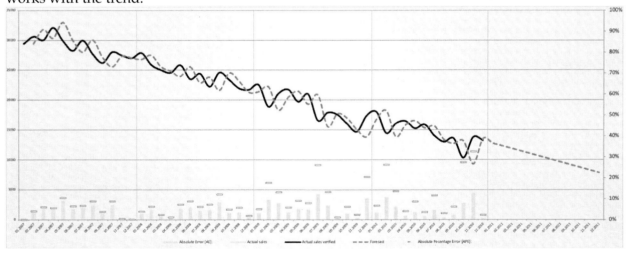

Figure 66 - Example of how the Moving Average Method works with the Trend for dwindling sales

EXAMPLE OF SPREADSHEET IMPLEMENTATION

Implementation of this method in the spreadsheet for the 3M moving average:

	A	B	C	D	E	F	G	H	I	J
2			t :	1	2	3	4	5	6	7
3	INPUT DATA		Year :	2007	2007	2007	2007	2007	2007	2007
4			Month :	1	2	3	4	5	6	7
5			Date :	Jan-07	Feb-07	Mar-07	Apr-07	May-07	Jun-07	Jul-07
6			Actual Sales :	29 428	30 629	30 054	32 112	29 905	28 240	29 979
8			Actual Sales Verified :	29 428	30 629	30 054	32 112	29 905	28 240	29 979
10			Forecast :		29 428	31 830	30 367	33 007	29 664	=I8+AVERAGE(G14:I14)
11	Forecasting	0,000								
12		0,000								
13		0,000								
14		0,000	Delta		1 201	-575	2 058	-2 207	-1 665	1 739

Figure 67 - Implementation of the Moving Average Method with the Trend for k=3

ISSUES RELATED TO APPLICATION OF THIS METHOD

It is a relatively useful method which allows to react to a change in the trend, however, depending on the number of k periods which determine the strength of the of the sales trend growth (or decline) in subsequent periods, this model's reaction to the trend change dynamics is varied. Quick responses to trend movements are enabled by the other methods described in here (Weighted Moving Average for the Trend, Exponential Smoothing).

Weighted Moving Average used with the Trend

Similarly to the aforedescribed Moving Average Method, this one also takes into account only a specific number of observations (k) which it includes when calculating sales forecasts for subsequent periods. However, it allows to manually assign weight to specific observations so that it is more reactive to the behaviour of the time series for the observed sales.

The following formulas are a formal representation of this method:

$$F_{t+h|t} = A_t + h \cdot \bar{\Delta}$$

where:

$$\bar{\Delta} = \frac{1}{k} \sum_{i=t-k+1}^{t} \omega_i \cdot (A_i - A_{i-1})$$

and

k – *number of included observations,*
ω_i – *weight of each included observation where $\sum \omega_i = 1$.*

The principle of this method is shown in this graph below.

If the time series shows rather frequent trend changes, giving a lot of weight to the last observation in the model allows to react to such situations much quicker.

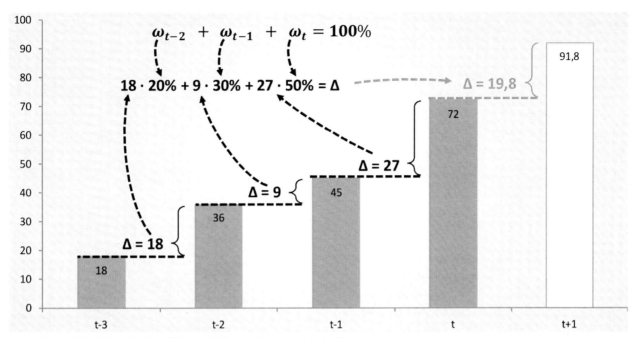

$$\omega_{t-2} + \omega_{t-1} + \omega_t = 100\%$$

$$18 \cdot 20\% + 9 \cdot 30\% + 27 \cdot 50\% = \Delta$$

$\Delta = 19{,}8$

$\Delta = 27$

$\Delta = 9$

$\Delta = 18$

91,8

72

45

36

18

t-3   t-2   t-1   t   t+1

Figure 68 - Principle of the Weighted Moving Average with the Trend

EXAMPLE OF THE METHOD APPLICATION
Presented in the chart below is how the method works:

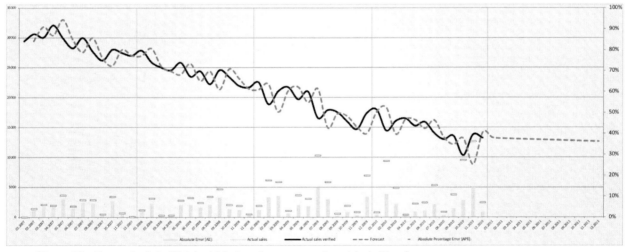

Figure 69 - Example of the Weighted Moving Average operating with the Trend

EXAMPLE OF SPREADSHEET IMPLEMENTATION
Presented hereunder is an example of the method's implementation in a spreadsheet:

	A	B	C	D	E	F	G	H	I	J
2			t :	1	2	3	4	5	6	7
3			Year :	2007	2007	2007	2007	2007	2007	2007
4			Month :	1	2	3	4	5	6	7
5			Date :	Jan-07	Feb-07	Mar-07	Apr-07	May-07	Jun-07	Jul-07
6	INPUT DATA		Actual Sales :	29 428	30 629	30 054	32 112	29 905	28 240	29 979
8			Actual Sales Verified :	29 428	30 629	30 054	32 112	29 905	28 240	29 979
10			Forecast :		29 428	31 830	30 367	33 007	29 664	=I8+AVERAGE(G14:I14)
11	Forecasting	0,000								
12		0,000								
13		0,000								
14		0,000	Delta		1 201	-575	2 058	-2 207	-1 665	1 739

Figure 70 - Implementation of the Weighted Moving Average for the Trend

ISSUES RELATED TO APPLICATION OF THIS METHOD

This method allows for a rather good forecasting of series showing trends, even the variable ones. Nonetheless, a large number of parameters (K and the dependent number of weights for individual past observations) cause it to be rather complicated and require – in order to use it effectively – a very sound knowledge of sales performance of a given product. It does, however, find its use in case of specific runs which require manual weight control, not possible in the Linear Exponential Smoothing Method described next.

Linear Exponential Smoothing Method

Holt's Linear Exponential Smoothing Method, also referred to as double exponential smoothing, is a method based on the same principles as the Simple Exponential Smoothing (SES) method, however, it is dedicated to time series showing a trend as next to the element responsible for forecasting an adequate level (L) an extra component has been introduced to the model, ensuring that the trend, changeable by assumption (T), is being followed.

Thus the method allows to lift the restrictions of the SES method where in case of series with a trend there has always been a delay. Moreover, the trends in the time series vary an similarly to the level of sales also the trend direction should be adequately adjusted.

As there is a second β parameter introduced in this method, responsible for regulating how quickly the trend adapts. As in the SES method, also here the weights of the trend component of time series diminish correspondingly to the growing '*age*' of observation of this trend.

Its mathematic representation is as follow:

$$F_{t+h|t} = L_t + T_t \cdot h$$

where:

L_t – *estimated Level (L) at time (t) calculated using this formula:*

$$L_t = \alpha \cdot A_t + (1 - \alpha)(L_{t-1} + T_{t-1})$$

→ *via analogy to the SES, where:*

$$F_{t+1} = \alpha \cdot A_t + (1 - \alpha) \cdot F_t$$

T_t – *estimated Trend (T) parameter at time (t), calculate according to the formula:*

$$T_t = \beta \cdot (L_t - L_{t-1}) + (1 - \beta) \cdot T_{t-1}$$

h – *forecast horizon expressed in a number of 'forward' periods*

α – *level smoothing parameter; $0 \leq a \leq 1$,*
β – *trend smoothing parameter; $0 \leq \beta \leq 1$,*
L_t-L_{t-1} – *difference in level estimates → observed trend,*
$L_{t-1} + T_{t-1}$ – *'old' calculation of the smoothed level together with the 'old' trend parameter → 'old' forecast.*

The principle of this method is best explained hereunder:

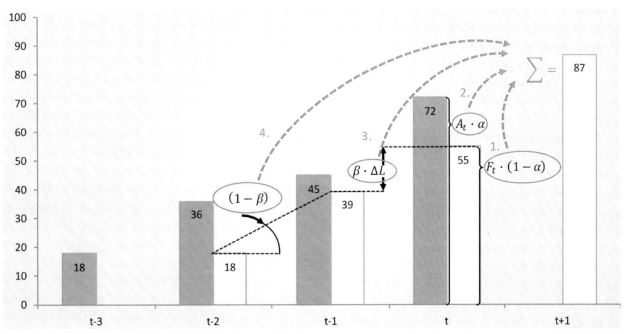

Figure 71 - Principle of Holt's Exponential Smoothing Method

As it stems from the above, there are four components which affect forecast calculation for another period:

- two components which depend on the level of the realized sales values (A_t) and the sales forecast (F_t) in the current period, multiplied by α parameter and, respectively, its complementary value (1-α),
- two components which depend on the value of trends observed in the current period and the preceding period, multiplied by parameter β and its complementary value (1- β).

Interpretation of parameters for both α and β model is identical as in the SES method:

- α smoothing parameter denotes the weight of the last sales level observation in an average in %,
- β smoothing parameter denotes the weight of the last trend observation in %,
- each smoothing parameter determines the strength of time series smoothing (by correspondence to other average methods of varied smoothing lengths),

- smoothing parameters denote the lengths of averages over a period of time.

The main undisputed advantages of this method include:

- no delays compared to the trend,
- faster adaptation to the trend fluctuations,
- faster adaptation to the sales level changes (and impulse sales – the so called outliers).

EXAMPLE OF THE METHOD APPLICATION

Figure 72 below shows how this method works with a real series of data:

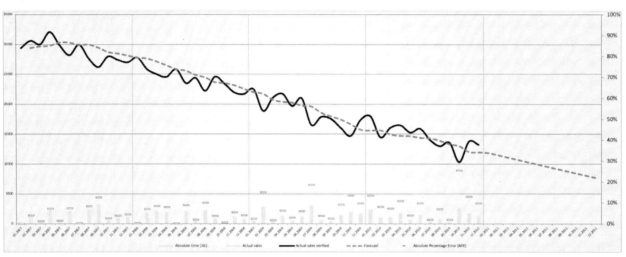

Figure 72 - Example of Holt's Method application

SPREADSHEET IMPLEMENTATION EXAMPLE

An example of implementation in a spreadsheet is presented at Figure 73 hereunder.

ISSUES RELATED TO APPLICATION OF THIS METHOD

Despite major advantages of this method, visible at a glance is its main disadvantage. Basically, with any trend, either decreasing or increasing, the forecast sales values will start adopting negative values over time (which is not possible other than in rare situations of the so called *returns*) or will grow indefinitely – although such situations would be a dream-come-true for any head of sales, business or brand owner, it is a piece of fiction nevertheless.

Thus, while introducing certain modifications accounting for this serious limitation, a development on this method has been introduced, offering a trend dampening parameter, preventing estimation of unrealistic forecasts. This modified method has been presented in the next section.

Some other problems with this method which may occur:

- if the parameters are not selected well, noises may be interpreted as fluctuations in trend,
- it requires 2 parameters, which increases
  - complexity of search for optimal parameters and
  - complexity of forecast estimation formulas.

Panel 1

	A	B	C	D	E	F	G	H
	INPUT DATA			t :	1	2	3	4	5
				Year :	2007	2007	2007	2007	2007
				Month :	1	2	3	4	5
				Date :	Jan-07	Feb-07	Mar-07	Apr-07	May-07
				Actual Sales :	29 428	30 629	30 054	32 112	29 905
				Actual Sales Verified :	29 428	30 629	30 054	32 112	29 905
	Forecasting			Forecast :		29 428	29 692	29 796	30 337
		0,200		Lt	29 428	29 668	29 765	=$B$11*G8+(1-$B$11)*(F11+F12)	30 250
		0,100		Tt		24,02	31,26		68,95
		0,000							
		0,000							

Panel 2

	A	B	C	D	E	F	G	H
	INPUT DATA			t :	1	2	3	4	5
				Year :	2007	2007	2007	2007	2007
				Month :	1	2	3	4	5
				Date :	Jan-07	Feb-07	Mar-07	Apr-07	May-07
				Actual Sales :	29 428	30 629	30 054	32 112	29 905
				Actual Sales Verified :	29 428	30 629	30 054	32 112	29 905
	Forecasting			Forecast :		29 428	29 692	29 796	30 337
		0,200		Lt	29 428	29 668	29 765	30 259	30 250
		0,100		Tt		24,02	31,26	=$B$12*(G11-F11)+(1-$B$12)*F12	68,95
		0,000							
		0,000							

Panel 3

	A	B	C	D	E	F	G	H
	INPUT DATA			t :	1	2	3	4	5
				Year :	2007	2007	2007	2007	2007
				Month :	1	2	3	4	5
				Date :	Jan-07	Feb-07	Mar-07	Apr-07	May-07
				Actual Sales :	29 428	30 629	30 054	32 112	29 905
				Actual Sales Verified :	29 428	30 629	30 054	32 112	29 905
	Forecasting			Forecast :		29 428	29 692	29 796 =G11+G12*1	
		0,200		Lt	29 428	29 668	29 765	30 259	30 250
		0,100		Tt		24,02	31,26	77,58	68,95
		0,000							
		0,000							

Figure 73 - Example of Implementation of the LES Method in a spreadsheet

Dampened Trend Exponential Smoothing

Dampened Trend Exponential Smoothing is a method which expands on the LES model, including a trend damping factor. This prevents, among others, the indefinite sales growth with an uptrend or forecasting negative sales values with a downtrend.

The principle of this method is not, as a rule, different than the LES method, other than an additional φ parameter which allows to regulate the trend damping strength.

A mathematic presentation of this method is provided hereunder, in the following formula:

$$F_{t+h|t} = L_t + \sum_{i=1}^{h}(\phi^i \cdot T_t)$$

where:

$$L_t = \alpha \cdot A_t + (1 - \alpha)(L_{t-1} + \phi \cdot T_{t-1})$$

$$T_t = \beta \cdot (L_t - L_{t-1}) + (1 - \beta) \cdot \phi \cdot T_{t-1}$$

Φ – trend damping factor, and when $|\phi| < 1$, the sales level comes close to the value set by the limit as presented below:

$$\lim_{h \to \infty}\left(\sum_{i=1}^{h}(\phi^i \cdot T)\right) = \frac{T}{1 - \phi}$$

The other elements of formulas have been described in the previous section on the LES method.

EXAMPLE OF THE METHOD APPLICATION

Examples of forecasts using this method are presented in the following graphs (downtrend for the same data as for the LES model and the same α and β parameters, i.e. α = 0.2 , β = 0.1, and φ = 0.95):

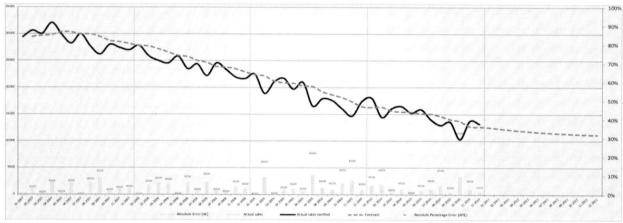

Figure 74 - Example of the DTES Method working with a downtrend where a = 0.2 and β = 0.1 and φ = 0.95

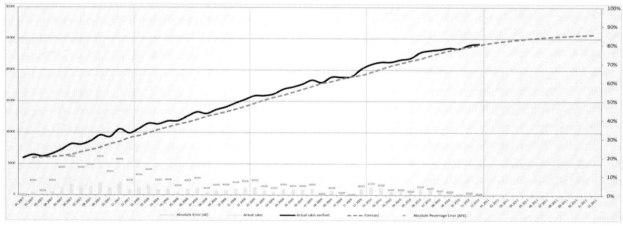

Figure 75 - Example of the DTES Method working with the uptrend where a = 0.2 and β = 0.1 and φ = 0.95

SPREADSHEET IMPLEMENTATION EXAMPLE

An example of the method's implementation in the spreadsheet is presented hereunder.

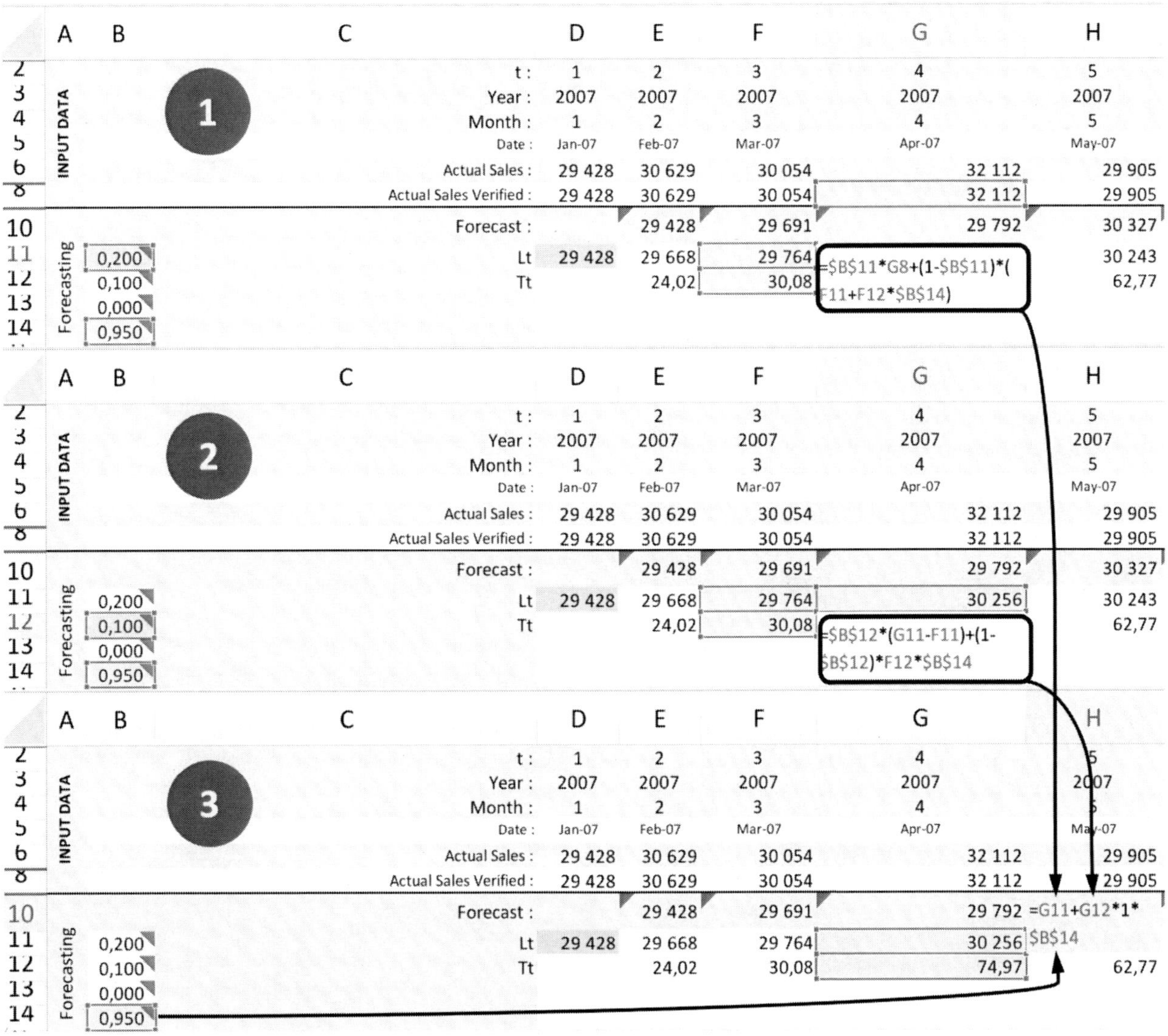

Figure 76 - Example of implementation of the DTES Method in a spreadsheet

Models for series showing seasonality

Similarly to stationary series and series showing a trend, it is possible to recall corresponding models based on averages. As seasonality is a more complex phenomenon which requires a rather comprehensive approach, this review quotes 2 methods which are opposite to one another when it comes to comprehensiveness of approach but nonetheless both find their application in practice.

A prerequisite for using the methods in respect of seasonal sales is access to the sales history for at least one full sales season (usually one year).

3rd type Naive Method

Naive Method for time series with a seasonality effect assumes that the sales level for the period subject to forecast will repeat sales execution for a corresponding period in the past season, e.g. the forecast developed in February for the upcoming April will repeat the sales from April recorded in previous year if we treat one year as a season and the months as periods subject to the forecast.

The formal record of this method is presented by the following formula:

$$F_{t+h|t} = A_{t+h-s}$$

where:

s – number of time units at time, namely if one year is the period and the sales execution and forecasts are developed with one month accuracy (s = 12), the formula is:

$$F_{t+1} = A_{t+1-12} = A_{t-11}$$

EXAMPLE OF THE METHOD APPLICATION

Examples of how this method works with the forecasts are presented hereunder. The first graph shows the result for a rather regular seasonality model:

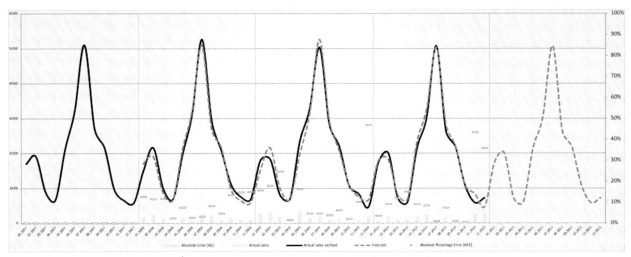

Figure 77 - Example of the 3rd Type Naive Model used in a forecast with a seasonality

While the other one shows an effect when sales comes as combination of seasonality and trend:

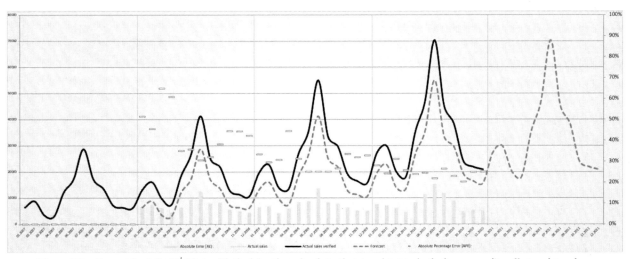

Figure 78 - Example of the 3rd Naive Method for the sales data that is subject to both the seasonality effect and trend

SPREADSHEET IMPLEMENTATION EXAMPLE

An example of implementation in the spreadsheet is shown hereunder:

	A	B	C	D	E	F	G	H	I	J	K	L	M	N	O	P	Q
2			t :	1	2	3	4	5	6	7	8	9	10	11	12	13	14
3			Year :	2007	2007	2007	2007	2007	2007	2007	2007	2007	2007	2007	2007	2008	2008
4		INPUT DATA	Month :	1	2	3	4	5	6	7	8	9	10	11	12	1	2
5			Date :	Jan-07	Feb-07	Mar-07	Apr-07	May-07	Jun-07	Jul-07	Aug-07	Sep-07	Oct-07	Nov-07	Dec-07	Jan-08	Feb-08
6			Actual Sales :	6 353	8 694	3 366	2 912	12 032	17 072	28 621	16 971	13 438	7 043	6 234	6 071	13 062	15 936
8			Actual Sales Verified :	6 353	8 694	3 366	2 912	12 032	17 072	28 621	16 971	13 438	7 043	6 234	6 071	13 062	15 936
10			Forecast :													6 353	=E8

Figure 79 - Example of implementation of the 3rd Naive Method in the spreadsheet

ISSUES RELATED TO APPLICATION OF THIS METHOD

As the presented examples clearly show the method may prove effective in practice but only in case of stable seasonal sales (the first graph). If apart from seasonality the sales are subject to additional phenomena such as a trend, this method cease to be effective.

Seasonal Exponential Smoothing Method

SnES (Seasonal Exponential Smoothing), also referred to as the Triple Exponential Smoothing or Winters Method, similarly to the LES Method is a development on the basic exponential smoothing method, however, it takes into consideration the seasonality element in the time series. To that end the element for identification and forecasting of a seasonality (S) factor has been introduced to the model. The idea behind this factor is the same as in the basic SES method.

This forecasting model generally requires observations from several most recent periods in full.

The underlying mechanism involves the first step, i.e. indexing the sales results generated over the entire period (year) as compared to the average for the entire period, namely calculating the so called seasonality index for each observed sales level over the entire period. This is shown in Figure 80 below.

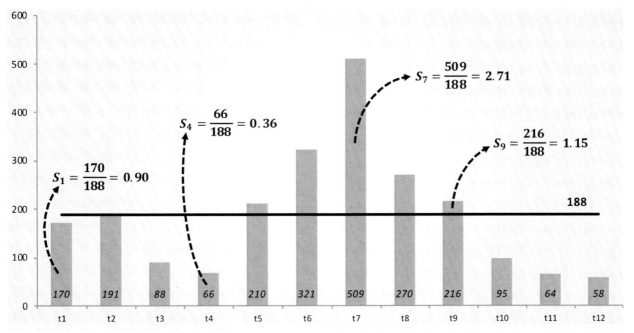

Figure 80 - Calculation of seasonality indices in the SnES model

This method assumes a relatively stable seasonality:

$$S_1 = \frac{A_1}{Average} = \frac{170}{188} = 0.90$$

...

$$S_4 = \frac{A_4}{Average} = \frac{66}{188} = 0.36$$

...

$$S_7 = \frac{A_7}{Average} = \frac{509}{188} = 2.71$$

...

Thus, each (monthly) sales realized over time (year) obtains an index which shows relative sales increase in a given period over the entire season.

After such indexing of all the historic sales results it is possible to juxtapose corresponding indices from the consequent full seasons. This is shown in Figure 81 below.

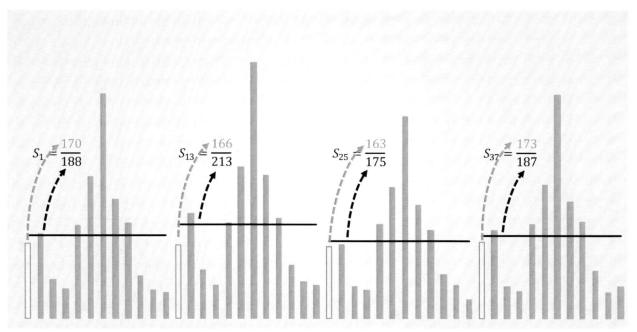

Figure 81 - Calculation of corresponding season indices for the consequent 4 seasons with seasons averaging, respectively 188, 213, 175 and 187

Then:

For the sales averages in subsequent seasons, amounting to 188, 213, 175 and 187, respectively, the seasonality indices for the first sales periods will be, respectively:

$$S_1 = \frac{A_1}{Avg_{seas1}} = \frac{170}{188} = 0.90$$

$$S_{13} = \frac{A_{13}}{Avg_{seas2}} = \frac{166}{213} = 0.78$$

$$S_{25} = \frac{A_{25}}{Avg_{seas3}} = \frac{163}{175} = 0.93$$

$$S_{37} = \frac{A_{37}}{Avg_{seas4}} = \frac{173}{187} = 0.93$$

With such historical indices at hand, for the specific sales periods over the past full periods, one may feel inclined to present the methods based on averages, corresponding to those discussed with stationary time series with a trend, selecting them and lending adequate weight to the individual indices. Nonetheless, as per earlier statement, we shall move straight away to discussing the Seasonal Exponential Smoothing.

In this model – through resemblance to the Brown's Method (refer to chapter *Brown Single Exponential Smoothing*, page 111) – the parameter responsible for the exponentially smoothed seasonality (S_t) is calculated, as one of the model's components, using γ parameter responsible for the 'strength' of smoothing of this factor:

$$S_t = \gamma \cdot \frac{A_t}{L_t} + (1 - \gamma) \cdot S_{t-s}$$

where:

$$L_t = \alpha \cdot \frac{A_t}{S_{t-s}} + (1 - \alpha) \cdot L_{t-1}$$

and

S_t – *seasonality component for the period (t)*,

s – *season's length in a number of periods (sales)*,

γ – *smoothing parameter for the season; $0 \leq \gamma \leq 1$*,

α – *smoothing parameter corresponding to SES/LES; $0 \leq a \leq 1$*,

Then the formula for the forecast's model is as follows:

$$F_{t+h|t} = L_t \cdot S_{t-s+h}$$

The principle of the model's operations for a full period divided into 12 sections is shown in the graph below. Noticeable already at the first glance is high complexity of calculations for the model. Interpretation of parameters in α and γ models is the same as in the SES and LES models:

- α smoothing parameter denotes the weight of the most recent observation for the sales level in average, expressed as %,
- γ smoothing parameter denotes the weight of the most recent seasonality index among the other ones (corresponding to the forecast one), expressed as %,
- each of the smoothing parameters determines the strength of the time series smoothing (via analogy to other average methods showing various smoothing length),
- smoothing parameters define the length of averages over time.

The definite advantages of this methods include:

- faster adaptation to fluctuations in the seasonality indices,
- faster adaptation to changes in the sales levels (and impulse sales).

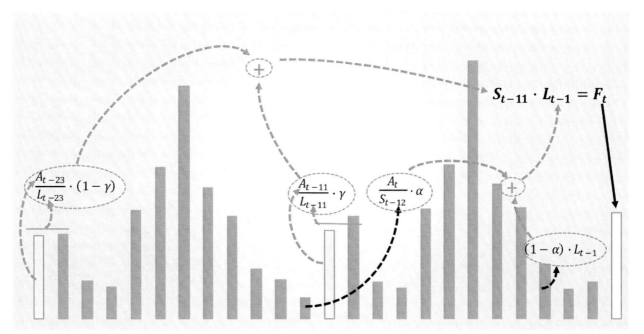

Figure 82 - Principle of the Seasonal Exponential Smoothing Method

EXAMPLE OF THE METHOD APPLICATION

An example of how this method works with historical data for 4 full periods and parameters α = 0.2 and γ = 0.4 is shown in the figure below:

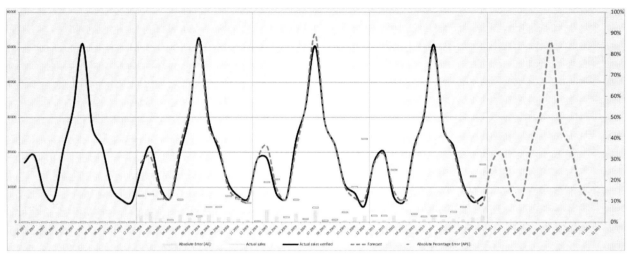

Figure 83 - Seasonal Exponential Smoothing Method for the historical data from 4 full periods and a = 0.2 and y = 0.4

SPREADSHEET IMPLEMENTATION EXAMPLE

An example of implementation in the spreadsheet is shown hereunder:

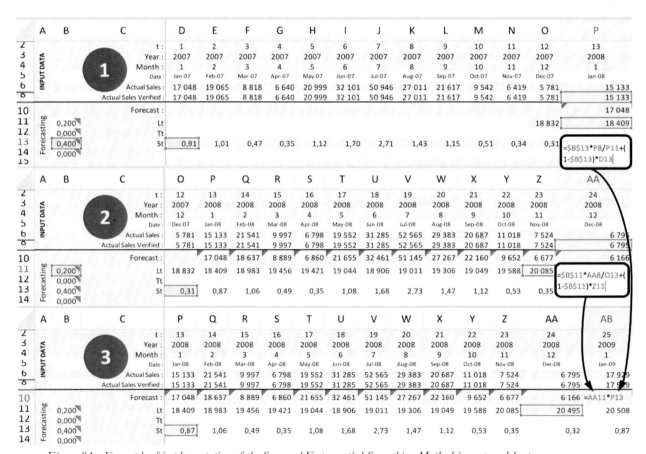

Figure 84 - Example of implementation of the Seasonal Exponential Smoothing Method in a spreadsheet

Disadvantage arising when using this method include foremostly:

- if inadequate parameters are selected, noises may be interpreted as fluctuations in seasonality indices,

- it requires 2 parameters and therefore:
  o searching for optimum parameters is hard and
  o forecast calculation formulas are rather complex and therefore time consuming.

Models for series showing trend and seasonality

When reviewing the methods related to time series, presented in previous sections, we may notice that they are sufficient to rather accurately forecast all the circumstances which affect sales on an everyday basis, namely the regular sale on a specific period, the regular sales combined with the impulse sales, change in the sales level, trend and seasonality effect. Still, in order to completely fill in the picture to include all the common phenomena and possible combinations thereof, we need to also describe a method allowing to forecast the sales and comprising both the trend component and the seasonality element. One of such methods is the Linear and Seasonal Exponential Smoothing.

Trend-Seasonal Exponential Smoothing

This method is also known as the Triple Exponential Smoothing or Holt-Winters Exponential Smoothing (from the names of its authors). It brings together the Linear and the Seasonal Exponential Smoothing Methods whose general principles have been set out in the earlier sections. Its mechanism is based on the Brown's Method idea, expanded to include all 3 components, i.e. the sales, the trend and the seasonality.

The mathematic formula for this model is as follows:

$$F_{t+h|t} = (L_t + T_t \cdot h) \cdot S_{t-s+h}$$

where:

$$L_t = \alpha \cdot \frac{A_t}{S_{t-s}} + (1 - \alpha) \cdot (L_{t-1} + T_{t-1})$$

$$S_t = \gamma \cdot \frac{A_t}{L_t} + (1 - \gamma) \cdot S_{t-s}$$

$$T_t = \beta \cdot (L_t - L_{t-1}) + (1 - \beta) \cdot T_{t-1}$$

and:

h – *planning horizon, presented as a number of periods (of sales),*

s – *length of period in a number of time series (of sales),*

α – *smoothing parameter for level; $0 \leq a \leq 1$,*

β – *smoothing parameter for trend; $0 \leq \beta \leq 1$,*

γ – *smoothing parameter for seasonality; $0 \leq \gamma \leq 1$.*

Interpretation of α, β and γ parameters is similar to the other methods of exponential smoothing:

- α smoothing parameter defines the weight of the most recent observation of the sales in an average,
- β smoothing parameter defines the weight of the most recent trend observation,
- γ smoothing parameter defines the weight of the most recent seasonality index from the other ones (corresponding to the forecast one),
- each of the smoothing parameters determines the strength of smoothing the time series (through analogy to other average methods of various smoothing lengths),
- the parameters specify the length of averages over time.

The advantages of using this method include the combined benefits of the aforedescribed methods based on exponential smoothing.

In case of this model it is hard to explain its principle based on illustrations for reference only. Therefore, all those interested in obtaining a better understanding of this method are advised to:

- study the LES and SnES methods once again and
- analyse the related formulas and data used in examples of implementation of those methods in the spreadsheets which allow to freely test and experiment with the discussed models using any other sets of data.

EXAMPLE OF THE METHOD APPLICATION

The following graph shows the use of this method:

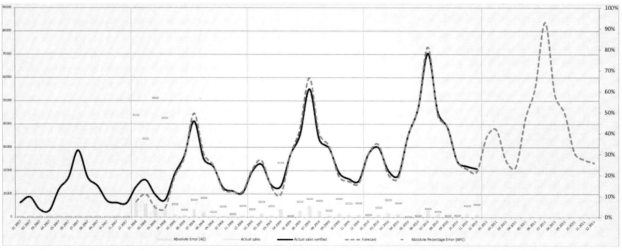

Figure 85 - Linear an Seasonal Exponential Smoothing Method used with the historical data for 4 full periods

SPREADSHEET IMPLEMENTATION EXAMPLE

Implementation of this model in the spreadsheet is shown in Figure 86 below.

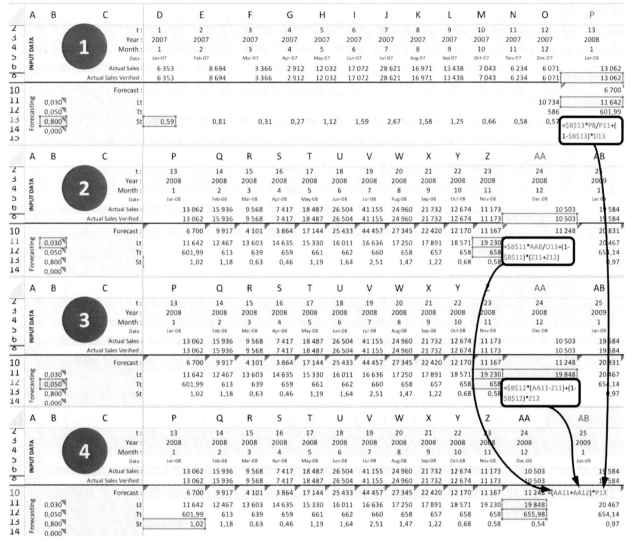

Figure 86 - Example of implementation of the Linear and Seasonal Exponential Smoothing Method in a spreadsheet

ISSUES RELATED TO THE USE OF THIS METHOD

Inconveniences which arise are similar to those specified when presenting methods based on exponential smoothing, to summarize:

- if the selected parameters are inadequate, the model may interpret noises as fluctuations of trend or seasonality indices,

- it requires 3 parameters and therefore:
  o you are faced with high complexity of searching for optimal parameters of the model and
  o forecast calculation formulas are very complicated for this method,
- additionally, in order to work appropriately the model requires historical data for at least 2 full periods.

Models for time series - Summary

The 'evolutionary' and rather extensive presentation describes models for stationary series and for series showing a trend. When indicating resemblance between methods for those two types of time series, it is possible to understand methods for seasonal time series and seasonal series with a trend without any assistance.

Nevertheless, as in case of stationary series and at times also series with a trend, it is possible to find application for each of the presented methods in a day's work, however, in case of seasonality an seasonality with trend – due to complexity – only the more advanced methods (usually the exponential smoothing methods) are used.

Here we may arrive at a conclusion that every new presented method is an improvement on those discussed earlier and generally it would be best to apply the most advanced methods (e.g. the exponential smoothing methods). There is a lot of sense to it, however, we must bear in mind that the persons in charge of forecasting deal on an everyday basis with hundreds if not thousands of products and the workload required should be in proportion to the quality of forecast obtained.

It should also be mentioned that even though the IT hardware and technologies are becoming ever more advanced, generating forecasts for the entire large product portfolio using more advanced methods is very resource consuming and by no means are they available at a moment's notice (at any given moment upon update of the entry data).

For that reason, aiming at maximum use of the system's resources, the simplest of models are used whenever possible. In many situations even some averages methods are sufficient as their updating in the systems supporting forecasting is much easier and faster as compared to implementation and maintenance of more advanced models, and the forecast obtained as a result are of comparative quality.

In case of much more complex phenomena such as seasonality an trend, application of more advanced models is advised as according to some common sense thinking the data from the most recent periods is the best basis for formulating forecasts for the next periods.

We should also bear in mind that the main objective of the discussed methods is to filter out the so called 'noises' and capture the main factors which determine the sales, i.e. the level of sales, trend and seasonality. Generally, we can recognize as 'noises' in the sales reality all the phenomena which cause deviation from the expected behaviour, such as for instance sudden sales peaks, unscheduled promotional activities of the competitors or own, launch of new products, untypical weather conditions, macroeconomic and social phenomena, etc.

Other than the presented methods, there are certainly also other ones that exist and the new ones (such as the double moving average, linear regressions an their improvements), used in everyday activities. They have not been presented here as – what has already been mentioned earlier – the intention of this guidebook is not to develop an exhaustive compendium of the forecasting methodology but to present proven and widely used methods, while explaining how they work so that they can be used straight away. This is in order to follow the forecasting law which stipulates not to use any methods that are not fully understood.

It goes without saying that professional forecasting should exclude the Naive Method used only as a benchmark for the other methods applied so as to measure their quality or effectiveness.

Selection of adequate forecasting method is determined by such factors as, among others, the phase in the product's lifecycle, brand strength, loyalty of consumers, complexity to the sales system, susceptibility to promotional activities and a host of other factors hard to enumerate as they depend on a given business specifics and the person in charge of forecasting should have a knowledge of them and constantly study them so as to include them as appropriate in forecasting.

Often the inexperienced forecasters pass by the phase of basic models and straight away try to use the advanced methods, i.e. the neural networks which can certainly be an excellent forecasting tool but:

1. require a thorough understanding of their principles,
2. and most of all, in order to operate as designed, must be fed a huge amount of historical data, allowing to 'train' it as appropriate (5-6 years is minimum).

For those reasons it is suggested to get to know and implement forecasting methods successively, starting from the simplest ones through to the most advanced ones. This way or other, the biggest leap in the forecast quality shall be visible after appropriate application of the simplest methods, especially if the organization has had no forecasting process previously in place.

To close our discussion of the most important forecasting methods used in business let us summarize which methods from the presented one should be used, in respect of which time series groups – this is shown in Figure 87 below.

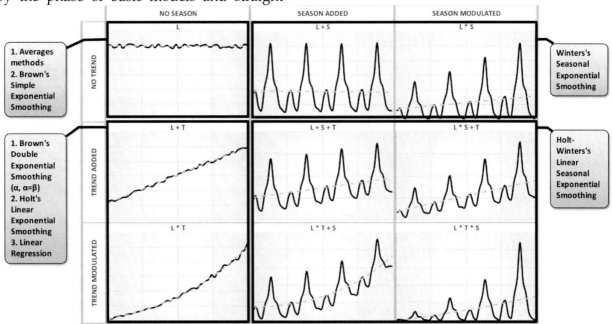

Figure 87 - Methods applied for individual time series types

6. Forecasting Quality Measurement

In this chapter...
- incentive to appropriately measure forecast quality, i.e. how the forecast quality measurement translates to business,
- forecast error vs. forecast accuracy,
- basic measures of forecast quality and measurements used in business.

Importance of forecast measurement accuracy in business

The related facts and findings of studies which show a direct relation between the forecast quality and the company's financial standing have been presented in the earlier chapters, especially the first one. And even though it is by no means a simple task to calculate at any given moment how much the company profits on every 1% of the forecast improvement, having read the earlier chapter the reader certainly realizes that improvement of the sales forecast pays off and by far!

The purpose of this chapter is not to prove this thesis yet again but to bring the reader closer to the issues related to quality of measurement of accuracy of the sales forecast, namely performing measurements so that their results are most exact at reflecting the status and accuracy of the processes related to forecasting.

Measurement of accuracy of the forecasts also allows to select and improve forecasting methodology so that the losses caused be erroneous forecasting can be minimized.

A well devised system for measurement of forecast quality enables quick identification of problematic areas both in terms of product and market (geographic areas, distribution channels, by Key Account, etc.), and it also helps to point out the main causes and help identify countermeasures.

In the context of the sales forecasting process and methodology it is not an area to be neglected and therefore it is worth to spend time on selecting methodology for the forecast quality measurement so that it is well thought out and optimal for a given organization.

Thus the issues tackled in this chapter include:

- review of methods which enable measurement of accuracy of the sales forecasts,
- practical application of those methods and how they are aggregated so that the measurement of the forecast quality at a cumulated level best presents their impact on business and helps identify problematic areas and undertake countermeasures.

Although it is not this book's intention to offer thorough knowledge of the statistical forecast quality measurement methods, it is unavoidable that some basic information from that area will be offered, allowing the reader to understand why certain methods may be used in their organization and the other one not, and what determines either case. The presented examples will offer a better understanding of those issues.

Basis

In the simplest formula forecast error E is a difference between the value (sales) realized and predicted, expressed as the following formula:

ERROR = ACTUAL - FORECAST

or another formal notation:

$$E_t = A_t - F_t$$

Often for the ease of interpretation absolute error AE is adopted an then the formal notation is as follows:

$$AE_t = |A_t - F_t|$$

where:
E_t – *forecast error over the period (t)*,
AE_t – *absolute forecast error over the period (t)*,
A_t – *real sales value, obtained during the period (t)*,
F_t – *sales forecast for the period (t)*.

Such information may seem rather trivial (and in fact it is trivial) but it is also the basis and a starting point for a review of the matter. The information is not trivial when part of everyday business reality, which is discussed in further sections. Forecast error is presented in Figure 88 below.

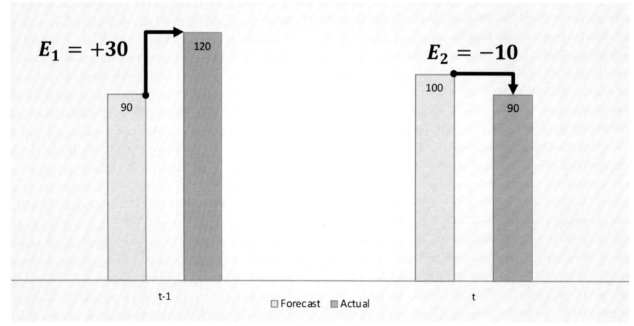

Figure 88 - Common forecasting errors: underestimation and overestimation

Apart from the specific value, this error also supplies information on whether it is a result of underestimation (positive value) or overestimation (negative value). Such information is true and shows real business consequences of making such error but only for a single observation. A question arises then: how to aggregate such two errors so that they still adequately show their business impact?

Underestimation with the value of 30 added to overestimation of -10 in the subsequent period, results in an underestimation of 20. When averaging those two values we get an underestimation of 10.

We are aware that both underestimating and overestimating is harmful to business and therefore adding or, what is even worse, averaging the errors, does not reflect

business losses.

In certain situations (e.g. errors in consequent periods with the values of -13, -10, 30, 25, -20, -12) the errors aggregated in this way may completely offset one another, showing that forecasting was perfect and 100% accurate during consequent periods... This is shown in Figure 89 below.

While looking only at a result of the error aggregated over time in this way, one could comment that business was not affected by erroneous forecasting, a statement which would obviously be false!

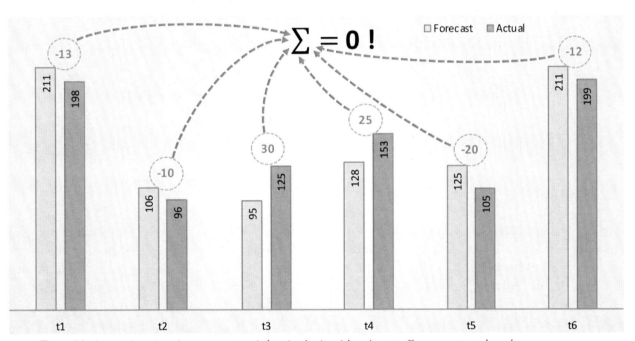

Figure 89 Aggregating errors in consequent periods using basic arithmetic may offer an unexpected result...

Forecast Accuracy vs. Forecast Error

Moving on to discuss correlation between forecast error and forecast accuracy expressed in relative terms (%) which are to

reflect forecasting quality: if we assume that the forecast error is a difference between the real performance (obtained / recorded and measured) and the forecast one, the forecast accuracy is its completion to the desired status, i.e. to 100%, as expressed by the following formula:

$$FCAcc_t = 100\% - E_t$$

As there are calculation formulas for certain types of errors where an error may exceed 100%, a mathematic formula facilitating interpretation of the forecast and, at the same time, protecting against forecast accuracy below 0% will be as follows:

$$FCAcc_t = Max\ (100\% - E_t,\ 0\%)$$

where:

FCAcc$_t$ – *forecast accuracy over time (t),*
E$_t$ – *forecast error over time (t).*

> In a business setting whenever we talk of forecast accuracy measurement we first of all think of error calculation and then deducting that error from 100%; for convenience of interpretation we express forecast accuracy of 0% to 100%.

Basic Measures of Forecast Quality

In this section we shall look at the basic measures of the sales forecasting quality, applied in business. In our discussion of the subject matter we should focus on not only the errors but also on how to present them on an aggregated level, allowing to appropriately interpret their impact on business.

Mean Error (ME)

Mean Error is an aggregation of individual errors using a simple arithmetic average. It is rather commonly used despite its basic fault which is offsetting of the component errors of opposite value ($\rightarrow$ refer to an earlier section).

Nonetheless, on the other hand, this form of error aggregation using the simplest arithmetic, i.e. adding and averaging, constitutes a great advantage thereof. An example of using this error is presented here in the Figure 90 below.

For the example shown in the picture the sum total of errors is 50 while the average value is 6.25. It can be stated in such circumstances that *over the examined period underestimation tendencies were recorded and*

an average forecast error for that period was 6.25. We can comment the aggregated error in this manner but NOTE: solely because we know the errors in individual periods and this comment stems not only from the averaged error for all the periods but also from observation of each component error alone.

In such circumstances such comment reflects the impact of forecasting errors on business with high probability. The formal mathematic notation of this form error is presented below:

$$ME_{t+n} = \frac{1}{n} \cdot \sum_{k=1}^{n} (A_{t+k} - F_{t+k})$$

where:

ME$_{t+n}$ – *mean forecast error for the period*

from t to t+n

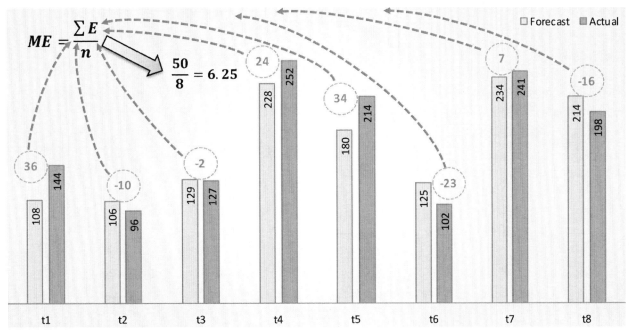

Figure 90 - Principle of calculation of the forecast Mean Error

We must remember that for error measurements without any clear overestimation or underestimation over a longer time, errors in plus and minus offset one another and then the Mean Error should be close to 0 – we must remember that when it comes to using this measure to evaluate forecast quality.

Just as this note is important when aggregating forecast errors over the time horizon of several periods, it should be similarly remembered when measuring forecast quality for a group of products.

In the view of the above one may also say that the Mean Error may be used to measure the bias in forecasts.

SUMMARY

PROs	CONs
• simple and comprehensible • common and easy to implement	• to a small degree it shows forecast error impact on business • component errors must be known in order to evaluate forecast quality
NOTES	
• may be used to measure the bias in forecasts	

Mean Square Error (MSE)

Mean Square Error naturally eliminates the Mean Error fault while bringing individual errors to positive values, thus enabling offsetting of plus and minus component errors.

Expressed as MSE with the following formula:

$$MSE_{t+n} = \frac{1}{n} \cdot \sum_{k=1}^{n} (A_{t+k} - F_{t+k})^2$$

where

MSE_{t+n} – *mean square error for the period from t to t+n.*

Its characteristic feature is that very strongly indicates (*'punishes'*) higher error values by square rooting them as its measure is an area of the square based on absolute value of the error as shown in Figure 91 below.

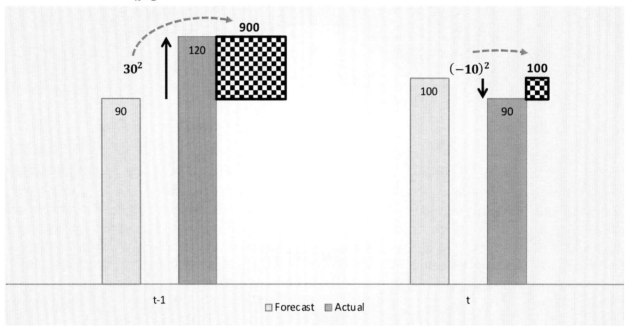

Figure 91 - Measure of square error is a square area where the side of the square equals an absolute value of the error

As it stems from the formula, the Mean Square Error is the average of areas of such squares, obtained over a given period (or for a specific product group, in case of aggregation to the level of product groups).

SUMMARY

PROs	CONs
• component overestimation and underestimation errors do not offset one another • comprehensible	• generates values in a nonlinear manner • hard to interpret and juxtapose – analysis of the entire portfolio is needed in order to find a reference point and the threshold of acceptable and nonacceptable values

NOTES
• useful when reporting in a business setting, when big errors generate disproportionally high financial losses comparing to small errors

Mean Absolute Error (MAE)

Mean Absolute Error (MAE) is another method to solve the problem where individual positive and negative errors offset on another when aggregated.

While calculating this error a difference between the recorded and forecast sales value is, as the first step, automatically brought down to an absolute value and then averaged.

Mean Absolute Error is expressed in the following formula:

$$MAE_{t+n} = \frac{1}{n} \cdot \sum_{k=1}^{n} |A_{t+k} - F_{t+k}|$$

where:

MAE_{t+n} – *Mean Absolute Error for the period from t to t+n.*

The principle for calculation of this error is shown in Figure 92 below – for the same data for which a common Mean Error was pictured earlier.

When using the Mean Absolute Error average forecast deviations from the obtained values are more exposed but at the same time we are losing any sense of whether the forecasting is balanced or shows a tendency for underestimation or overestimation.

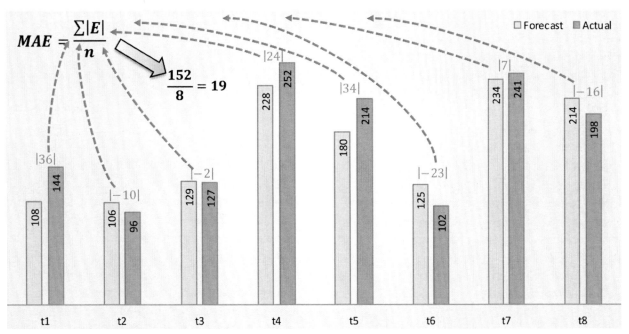

Figure 92 - Principle of calculation of the forecast Mean Absolute Error

SUMMARY

PROs	CONs
• simple and comprehensible • common • aggregates the impact of errors on business rather well regardless of whether they result from underestimation or overestimation	• no threshold for acceptable and unacceptable error levels • no sense of forecast bias

NOTES
• it can be used with less complex forecast error aggregation but it requires some business sense as to when the error becomes unacceptable

Mean Absolute Percentage Error (MAPE)

Mean Absolute Percentage Error abbreviated MAPE is an aggregated measure which allows to relativize and juxtapose forecast errors for various product categories and in various periods.

This measure is a solution of a common issue which arises in business, related to a question whether overestimation or underestimation by the same amount means a loss of the same weight for the business? This is clearly a rhetorical question as overestimation (or underestimation) of product A, sold in 100 000 units, by 100 units is different than in case of B product which was sold in 1000 units – in the first case it is a 0.1% error, while in the latter it is a 10% error.

Thus, the calculations should not be linked to value of the analysed feature and errors should be shown in relative terms – as a percentage. This may be aided by the percentage error.

A simple percentage error is presented in the following formula:

$$PE_{t+n} = \frac{1}{n} \cdot \sum_{k=1}^{n} \left(\frac{A_{t+k} - F_{t+k}}{A_{t+k}} \right)$$

However, when analysing the errors referred to earlier, the reader may straight away indicate the undesired characteristics and interpretation problems when there are different sets of data. Therefore, it is not subject to any wider discussion here. Instead, often used to measure forecast quality is Mean Absolute Percentage Error, expressed in the following formula:

$$MAPE_{t+n} = \frac{1}{n} \cdot \sum_{k=1}^{n} \left| \frac{A_{t+k} - F_{t+k}}{A_{t+k}} \right|$$

where

MAPE$_{t+n}$ – *mean absolute percentage error for the period from t to t+n.*

It is calculated as illustrated hereunder in Figure 93.

This type of error is rather commonly measured, however, it is still not free from certain inconveniences which hinder its interpretation. First of all, its formula does not work when the actual sales value is 0 – it is necessary to apply a solution which takes into account such an unusual situation.

Another situation which causes interpretation problems is when there is a very low sales value obtained with a given forecast level – then such error adopts values which are very hard to interpret, i.e. the sales averaged 91 and therefore the forecast was 91, while the actual sales delivered was 1 – in such case MAPE error equals 9000%!

Here are the methods used in practice to avoid such situations:

• calculating the mean while excluding any

extreme observations (e.g. 10% of the highest and 10% of the lowest forecast errors are excluded from calculation of the average),

• using the median instead of the mean as a result of the error measure (refer to the next section).

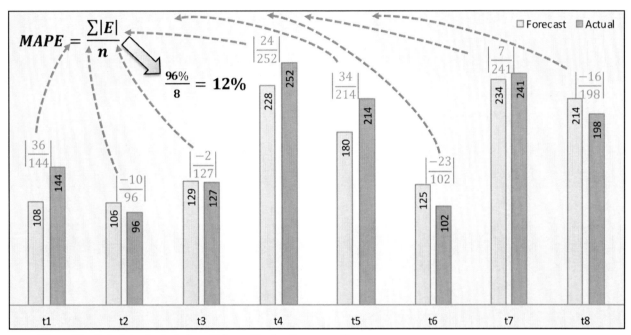

Figure 93 - Principle of calculation of Mean Absolute Percentage Error

As it stems from the above, the MAPE error is a rather convenient tool, however, only when the values obtained do not vary greatly from the mean value, otherwise the MAPE error values become hard to interpret.

SUMMARY

PROs	CONs
• relativization of results which enables juxtaposing various product groups in various aggregation measures • common applications	• inconvenient calculations when sales values recorded are 0 • difficult interpretation when extremely low sales results are obtained
NOTES	
• one of the more common methods for determining forecast quality	

Median Absolute Percentage Error (MdAPE)

Application of the Median Absolute Percentage Error – as already mentioned in the previous section – is one of the methods of avoiding an error with a value which is difficult in interpretation (as in case of MAPE).

It is generated by way of organizing all the recorded single errors in an increasing order and then selecting the middle value from the set organized in this manner as the end result (when the number of analyzed errors is uneven) or calculating an arithmetic average of the 2 middle observations (when the number of analyzed errors is even).

Formal notation of the Median Absolute Percentage Error is shown by the following formula:

$$MdAPE_{t+n} = Med_{k=t}^{t+n}\left(\left|\frac{e_k}{A_k}\right| * 100\right)$$

where

MdAPE$_{t+n}$ – *median absolute percentage error for the period from t to t+n.*

The principle for setting such error is presented in Figure 94 below.

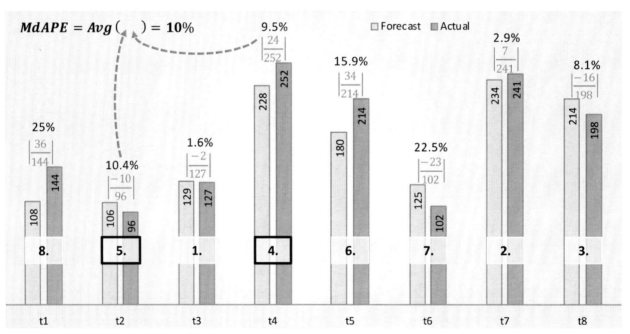

Figure 94 - Setting the Median Absolute Percentage Error

Other types of error measurement used in business

Other error measures used in the sales forecasting and planning processes are:
- **Root Mean Squared Error** used in place of the MSE in order to proportionally

reduce its values so as to render them easier to juxtapose. It is noted and described in the following manner:

$$RMSE_{t+n} = \sqrt{\frac{1}{n} \cdot \sum_{k=1}^{n} (A_{t+k} - F_{t+k})^2}$$

where
RMSE$_{t+n}$ – *root mean squared error for the period from t to t+n.*

- **Median Squared Error** described in the following manner:

$$MdSE_{t+n} = Med_{k=t}^{t+n}((e_k)^2)$$

where
MdSE$_{t+n}$ – *median squared error for the period from t to t+n,*

- **Symmetric Mean Absolute Percentage Error** used instead of MAPE due to the feature which allows to restrict its range from top and bottom; it is noted and described using one of the following 2 methods:

$$SMAPE_{t+n} = \frac{1}{n} \cdot \sum_{k=1}^{n} \frac{|A_{t+k} - F_{t+k}|}{(A_{t+k} + F_{t+k})/2}$$

or

$$SMAPE_{t+n} = \frac{1}{n} \cdot \sum_{k=1}^{n} \frac{|A_{t+k} - F_{t+k}|}{A_{t+k} + F_{t+k}}$$

where
SMAPE$_{t+n}$ – *symmetric mean absolute percentage error for the period from t to t+n.*

There are also other methods of measuring forecast error, however, since this publication is not designed to discuss all the known and used quality measures, they have been excluded on purpose and all those interested in widening their knowledge in this regard will certainly find the required information in the dedicated literature. This book is rather aimed at presenting the most important methods and pointing out their strengths and weaknesses so that the most adequate method for the organization may be selected, at least at the stage of implementing the forecasting process.

Apart from selection of a type of error to evaluate the forecast quality, also the issues discussed in the next section represent a challenge.

Measurement of forecast quality in a business setting

Following a brief review of the forecast error measures in the previous section, we can move on to forecast error measurement practice in a business setting. This is because certain problems arise that require the forecast quality reporting system to be tuned to the business needs.

The approaches referred to in here allow to appropriately report the errors aggregated both over time and in categories when the product portfolio is rather uniform (in terms of importance for the organization) and when the product portfolio is strongly diverse but it is still necessary to aggregate those errors so as to objectively measure the impact of those forecasts' quality on the organizations financial standing.

An important aspect to be taken into account is appropriate selection of the forecasts' horizons. They should be selected so that their measurement is not only appropriate as to the merit but also logical and justified from the business point of view.

Aggregating errors over time or in categories

Aggregating errors over periods is not really difficult as it basically comes down to calculation of sum totals of individual facts and the aggregated error values, and later the forecast accuracy, are calculated for those sum totals.

It is only important to bear in mind that while aggregating the forecast values all the component value be offered for the same forecasting horizons (e.g. M3), as discussed further in the section *Time horizons for forecast errors* (page 158). The manner of aggregating errors over time (e.g. monthly MAPE in a quarterly fashion) is shown in Figure 95 hereunder.

	B	C	D	E	F
2	*Facts \ Periods*	*Jan*	*Feb*	*Mar*	*Q1*
3	Actual	14 000	7 000	21 000	42 000
4	M3 Forecast	9 000	15 000	19 000	43 000
5	Absolute Error	5 000	8 000	2 000	15 000
6	Absolute Percentage Error	36%	114%	10%	=F5/F3
7	Forecast Accuracy	64%	0%	90%	64%

Facts \ Periods	*Jan*	*Feb*	*Mar*	*Q1*
Actual	14 000	7 000	21 000	42 000
M3 Forecast	9 000	15 000	19 000	43 000
Absolute Error	5 000	8 000	2 000	15 000
Absolute Percentage Error	36%	114%	10%	36%
Forecast Accuracy	64%	0%	90%	64%

Figure 95 - Quarterly aggregation of the monthly MAPE errors

We should remember all along that if we continue to aggregate over time, i.e. in half-annums or years, we should use basic values rather than the processed values, i.e. to calculate an aggregated annual value we should use the values from individual months rather than the quarterly data derived previously from months.

Aggregation of errors within the product category is similar, as shown in Figure 96 below. Similarly to aggregation of errors over time, when aggregating errors in specific categories, and then product groups or brands, there is a principle of using the basic data, and not the processed data, in calculation of error.

The method shown for aggregation of errors in a category is justified when individual products within the portfolio have the same importance for the company,

which does not happen often (as the Pareto principle is observed in nature), hence when aggregating errors in the category a different approach is taken, as discussed in the next section.

	B	C	D	E	F	G
1	Facts \ SKUs	Product A	Product B	Product C	Product D	Total Products Aggregated
2	Actual	500	1 000	1 500	1 480	4 480
3	M3 Forecast	1 500	0	500	1 500	3 500
4	Absolute Error	1 000	1 000	1 000	20	3 020
5	Absolute Percentage Error	200%	100%	67%	1%	=G4/G2
6	Forecast Accuracy	0%	0%	33%	99%	33%

Facts \ SKUs	Product A	Product B	Product C	Product D	Total Products Aggregated
Actual	500	1 000	1 500	1 480	4 480
M3 Forecast	1 500	0	500	1 500	3 500
Absolute Error	1 000	1 000	1 000	20	3 020
Absolute Percentage Error	200%	100%	67%	1%	67%
Forecast Accuracy	0%	0%	33%	99%	33%

Figure 96 - Aggregation of the MAPE errors for individual SKU as part of a category

Weighted errors in a product category

Let's analyse a simple situation when we are selling 2 products, A and B, and product A represents on average 2/3 of our sales value, while product B represents the remaining 1/3, and over the period in question the absolute AE forecast error for product A was 1 000 (with the realized sales value of 10 000), while for product B these values are respectively: AE – 2 000 and the realized sales value – 5 000.

With a simple approach the MAPE

forecast error for all of our products should be 25% (as a common average of the component errors). However, a question arises whether such approach reflects real damages to our business. The question is rhetorical in nature and the obvious answer is *NO!*

In this situation, it is natural to calculate the error reflecting *business damage* while adopting a weighted mean instead of an arithmetic one. Then it will make more sense to adopt for our products the weighted aggregated error MAPE, noted and calculated according to the following formula:

$$WMAPE_{A+B} = \frac{(AE_A \cdot w_A + AE_B \cdot w_B)}{(A_A \cdot w_A + A_B \cdot w_B)}$$

where

w_A *and* w_B *are the weights (of importance) of A and B products to our business.*

If in our example we treat as weights the percentage share of sales of individual

products, the aggregated error calculated according to this formula will be as follows:

$$WMAPE_{A+B} = \frac{(1\,000 \cdot 67\% + 2000 \cdot 33\%)}{(10\,000 \cdot 67\% + 5\,000 \cdot 33\%)} = 16\%$$

which is intuitively closer to the impression of *'damages'* suffered by the business due to the forecast errors committed for each of the products.

Aggregation method is shown in the Figure 97 here below:

	B	C	D	E	F
1	Facts \ SKUs	Product A	Product B	Total Products Aggregated	
2	Actual Sales Value	10 000	5 000		
3	M3 Sales Value Forecast	11 000	7 000		
4	Absolute Error	1 000	2 000		
5	Absolute Percentage Error	10%	=(C4*C6+D4*D6)/(C2*C6+D2*D6)		
6	Sales Value Share as a product relevance weight	67%	33%		
7	Forecast Accuracy	90%	60%	84%	
8					
	Facts \ SKUs	Product A	Product B	Total Products Aggregated	
	Actual Sales Value	10 000	5 000		
	M3 Sales Value Forecast	11 000	7 000		
	Absolute Error	1 000	2 000		
	Absolute Percentage Error	10%	40%	16%	
	Sales Value Share as a product relevance weight	67%	33%		
	Forecast Accuracy	90%	60%	84%	

Figure 97 - Aggregation of products within a category, accounting for their importance

In a business setting, the following values are accepted as weights for the individual component errors:
- sales value,
- sales volume,
- margin value,
- margin percentage,
- product manufacturing cost,
- product stocking cost,
- general logistic costs of the product, etc.

In practice, selecting the value to represent the product's weight (measure of its importance) is determined by which business area of the organization loses the most due to forecast errors or, in other words, which is a priority for the organization.

In case of accepting the sales volume, value or margin as the product's weight,

there is an inconvenience of fluctuations in these values over time, hence mean values are accepted for the past periods or the values planned for the current financial year.

Aggregation of the weighted errors over time

Reporting accuracy of forecasts as one of the KPIs requires aggregation of errors on a high level and for longer periods (e.g. as a temporary target for either a part of or the entire product portfolio). Therefore it is important to aggregate to the level of a brand, product category or even the entire portfolio over long periods so that this indicator is a real reflection of efficiency of actions aimed at improvement for forecasting quality.

The issues discussed in previous sections aid understanding to aggregation of the weighted forecast errors at a brand, category or product group level over longer periods, which takes place in the reporting systems of companies measuring them and accounting for them.

Such calculations boil down to calculation of the weighted error (e.g. WMAPE) for all the individual component periods and for all the products with appropriate weights. Mathematical notation is presented in the

following formula:

$$WMAPE_{A+N,t+n} = \frac{\sum_{k=1}^{n} \sum_{X=A}^{N} \left(AE_{X,k} \cdot w_X \right)}{\sum_{k=1}^{n} \sum_{X=A}^{N} \left(A_{X,k} \cdot w_X \right)}$$

where

WMAPE$_{A+N, t+n}$ – *aggregated weighted mean absolute percentage error for a groups of products from A to N and over a period from t to n,*

AE$_{X, k}$ – *absolute error for product X over period k,*

A$_{X, k}$ – *value of sales generated by product X over period k,*

w$_X$ – *X product weight.*

Presented below is calculation of the WMAPE for two products A and B in Q1 based on monthly results.

Calculations for a higher number of products and longer periods are performed correspondingly.

	Facts \ Periods	Jan	Feb	Mar	Q1
Product A	Actual	14 000	7 000	21 000	42 000
	M3 Forecast	9 000	15 000	19 000	43 000
	Absolute Error	5 000	8 000	2 000	15 000
	Cost of Product (CoP) as its relevance weight :				$ 4,50
	Absolute Percentage Error	36%	114%	10%	36%
	Forecast Accuracy	64%	0%	90%	64%
Product B	Actual	2 000	7 000	29 000	38 000
	M3 Forecast	9 000	15 000	19 000	43 000
	Absolute Error	7 000	8 000	10 000	25 000
	Cost of Product (CoP) as its relevance weight :				$ 1,50
	Absolute Percentage Error	350%	114%	34%	66%
	Forecast Accuracy	0%	0%	66%	34%

$$\text{WMAPE}_{(A+B,\ Q1)} = 43\% \rightarrow$$

=(E5*H6+F5*H6+G5*H6+E12*H13+F12*H13+G12*H13)/(E3*H6+F3*H6+G3*H6+E10*H13+F10*H13+G10*H13)

Figure 98 - Calculation of the WMAPE for products on a quarterly basis

Time horizons for forecast errors

Majority of the previously presented formulas for calculation of errors show how to make calculations for the forecasts with a horizon of 1 period (1 month – M1). If the errors are calculated for other horizons (M2, M3, M6…), which usually takes place, it is important to be aware of that and appropriately adjust formulas so that they unanimously specify the forecast horizons which a given calculation is based on.

This formula for calculation of the MAPE unanimously shows that 3 month (M3) forecasts have been used:

$$MAPE_{t+n} = \frac{1}{n} \cdot \sum_{k=1}^{n} \left| \frac{A_{t+k} - F_{t+k}^{M3}}{A_{t+k}} \right|$$

We must ensure that the measure of forecast quality (error) reflects the business damage suffered and therefore the forecast horizon should be the period which the lead-times are related to, i.e. certain technological or organizational restrictions which in a time shorter than the specific lead-time enable reorganization of the production or logistics process (in general: the chain of supplies process) in order to adjust the ability to supply a given product to the market to the observed change in demand for that product.

For instance, if the technological process for manufacturing a certain product requires it to be produced for 5 years and then shelved for 6 weeks, then with the preparations for production, packing, quality assurance and other necessary preparations for sales, its lead-time is ca. 2 months – in other words: after the production process starts the demand for that product cannot be decreased without incurring financial losses. Similarly, a month before the planned sales the order cannot be doubled as it is technologically unrealistic to produce it at such short notice.

Correspondingly, there are lead-times which result from logistic limitations: if the product sold on a given market is manufacture in other geographical regions (continents, parts of the world), excluding the time required for the production process, there is also the time needed to transport an appropriate volume of the specific product to the target market, which using a standard sea shipment may take e.g. 8-16 weeks.

There is a nonstandard transport available of course (e.g. by air) but it is more expensive, which is in the end reflected in the product's costs and, what follows, the financial performance. This discussion does not take into account the instances justified in business when such solutions are used (e.g. significant contractual damages, etc.) but those are still rare cases and not every product may be used in this way.

IN A NUTSHELL
- lead-time is a period when the organization has a limited ability to change the product volume supplied to the product market,
- for the forecast quality to be justified in business terms, the time horizons for which the forecasts are developed and their quality measured should be appropriately linked to the lead-times.

Forecast Quality Measure - Summary

In business it is important for the ales forecast quality measure best reflect the losses incurred by the organization due to forecasting errors. Thus, it is highly important to select the method which best fulfils this task in specific conditions of the organization.

It is not necessary or even recommended to use a higher number of error definitions to measure quality of the forecasting process.

In a business setting, it is sufficient to use 2 categories of indicators for measurement and adjustment of the sales forecast quality:

1. aggregated **absolute error indicator** which can be for instance MAP or WMAPE, a measure of the losses incurred by the company regardless of whether caused by under or overestimation and

2. forecast **bias indicator** which may be e.g. a common E or ME error, which when appropriately aggregated (correspondingly to WMAPE) shall reflect the bias of the process and enable the necessary corrective measures to be undertaken.

Especially valuable are long-term bias studies for a number of product subcategories, sales channels or geographical regions as if the observations show such bias (usually unveiling the internal interest of various employee groups), it allows to almost automatically adjust future forecasts and offers arguments to reach a compromise during the Consensus Meetings (refer to chapter *4. Sales Forecasting Process* page 59).

7. Summary, First Steps and Some More Afterwards

In this chapter...
- forecasting at a company... how to start?
- algorithm for implementation of the forecasting process,
- further steps improving the process.

Where the forecasting begins

Now then, after the reader has become acquainted with the major issues related to the forecasting process and methodology, they may decide which of the presented elements of the forecasting process are already in place at their organization and in what scope, and which require a review, a different approach or implementation completely from scratch.

Before any decision I suggest preparing a checklist with questions allowing to diagnose the situation at a given organization.

All the questions must be treated as open questions and we should aim at answering them in the most descriptive manner possible. In case of doubt regarding any of them, we should not hesitate to invite people from other departments who will be able to support us with their knowledge and experience.

Now then:

- What is the level of awareness of top executives regarding the relevance of the forecasting process and its impact on the company's financial performance?
- How do the managers of the trade departments (Sales, Marketing) perceive the significance of the forecasting process to their respective departments and the company as a whole?
- Are the sales plans and the operational plans (SOP) based on one and the same sales forecast, developed at one place of the organization? Or are the operational plans of individual departments base on the sales forecasts generated independently at a number of different places at the company?

- What is the frequency of meetings when the sales plans and the operational plans (i.e. production and logistics plans) are reviewed on an ongoing basis? Are these meetings perceived as productive? Are their participants the decision makers?
- Are the top executives, and if yes how, involved in decision making as part of this process?
- Is there a dedicated function within the organization (person or team) in charge of generation an consultation of the sales forecasts? If yes, which department does this person/team represent?
- How does the position of this person/team within the organization's structure and hierarchy guarantee lack of bias and objectivity in the process of development and consultation of the sales forecasts?
- Which discretions and authorizations of this person or team leader render him/her suitable to hold the position regarding the sales forecasts on par with the managers of the trade departments and the supply chain?
- How does the formal fixing of this function within the organization's hierarchy give it authority to moderate discussion with those managers and, on par with them, question, negotiate an consult the sales forecasts and the operational plans?
- To what extent does the incentive system operated at the company include the indicators related to the sales forecast quality?
- Which methods and models are used when generating and updating the

statistical sales forecasts?

- What types of sales are practiced at the company? What part of products is sold as part of these practices? How is the forecasting process and methodology adapted to those types of sales?
- In what way does the forecasting process account for the plans, forecasts or positions of the company's customers or suppliers?
- How often are the sales forecasts updated?
- How is the approach to forecasting for the individual product groups differentiated within the statistical forecasting process? Are they treated similarly?
- What criteria determine adjustment of the forecasting models to the individual products? How is it monitored whether the selection of those models is optimal?
- How are the parameters of the forecasting models selected? How often is the optimal selection of those parameters monitored?
- What methods are used to measure quality of the generated sales forecasts?
- How is the level of accuracy (quality) of the sales forecasts reported and

documented? How frequent is such monitoring?

- In which way is the forecasting process related to the other key business areas of the organization (apart from the operational planning)?
- How is the issue of synchronizing qualitative and quantitative forecasts resolved?

If majority of those questions can be answered, it means that it is possible to quickly make decisions or recommend changes in a given organization, relate to implementation or development of the forecasting process and improvement of its efficiency.

However, if the answers *Hard to say...* or *I don't know* prevail, it means that it is necessary to hold a certain number of meetings allowing to prepare to answer those questions.

No sooner than after finding the answers to at least the majority of those questions are you encouraged to read the next chapter on the implementation algorithm or the forecasting process improvement algorithm.

Forecasting Implementation Algorithm - Step by Step

Having collected the basic information on the functioning of key processes generating added value at the organization, and perhaps on the forecasting and operational planning as well, a decision may be taken to implement or develop the forecasting process. Presented below is the implementation algorithm, however, not all of its steps must refer to a given organization. It is subject to individual conditions and the current advancement of the forecasting process.

Nonetheless, regardless of which steps of

the algorithm refer to a given company and which do not, it is important to keep their sequence. Therefore:

1. Diagnose the level of awareness of the process' relevance. If necessary, either enhance it or build it. Without general understanding among the middle and top executives of how much the organization benefits from forecast quality improvement, you will not find the support necessary to implement this process. Therefore:

1.1.   If the forecast quality is measured, potential profits or savings may be estimated and shown (expressed in $) thanks to its improvement (see chapter *Importance of Forecasting in Business* page 14).

1.2. If the forecast quality has not yet been measured or is measured in the manner which prevents such calculations, check and estimate (quantify) in $:

1.2.1. How many products have become overdue, removed from the market and damaged as a result of inappropriate production or sales planning?

1.2.2. How many promotional offers have not been sold as scheduled due to delays in supply of promotional products to customers?

1.2.3. How many products have been damaged due to surplus (unnecessary) transport between distribution hubs?

1.2.4. What losses of product margins have been recorded by the company as a result of their sale before their due date?

1.2.5. What costs have been incurred by the company as a result of servicing returned or defective products?

1.2.6. What additional costs have been incurred by the company due to the need to supply materials, components or semi-finished goods, in a nonstandard fashion (e.g. by airmail)?

1.2.7. What was the customer service level?

1.2.8. What was the OOS level, i.e. the level of product shortages at the distributors' and on shop shelves?

1.2.9. How many times have the production lines been reorganized due to unavailability of components, materials or semi-finished goods?

1.2.10. What has been an average level of inventory of the ready goods?

1.2.11. What has been an average level of inventory of raw materials, materials, components and semi-finished goods, respectively?

1.2.12. Other issues arising from and related to production of or supply to customers of too many products or their temporary shortages arising from a low forecast quality.

1.3. Present the findings of your analyses to top executives (GM/CEO, Finance, Sales, Marketing, Logistics, Procurement) and gain their approval to the forecasting process implementation / improvement.

2. Perform the following analyses:

2.1. product portfolio (A-B-C, X-Y-Z, N-R-W, S-T-U);

2.2. analysis of the regular sales (fixed, showing a trend, seasonal), and irregular;

2.3. review them in the context of product life cycles (PLC) of individual products;

2.4. define the components of the sales performed via the specific distribution channels for individual groups of goods (regular sales, NPD/promotion).

3. Divide the product portfolio into categories (classes) of products an review the product portfolio and then:

3.1. Propose optimum forecasting level (SKU, index, etc.);

3.2. Initially select optimum forecasting methods or statistical forecasting method for each product within the portfolio.

3.3. Set the level of authority for the methods of forecasting, control and monitoring of quality of obtained forecast for the specific produced classes.

4. Determine how time consuming are the product portfolios required for forecasting and next determine the optimal number of the team responsible for the forecasting process.

5. Perform implementation of the process based on the forecasting cycle defined in the upcoming steps:

5.1. Verify the factors that impact the forecast size of demand and which factors bring the demand forecast to the sales forecast.

5.2. Check what are the lead-times for the products manufactured/ distributed by the organizations,

5.3. Select adequate forecasting levels and horizons adequate to realities and the organization's needs;

5.4. Check which forecast information exchange model and the operational plan the company cooperate with the contractor (suppliers or receivers).

5.5. Specify which organizational departments may supply the data/ information necessary to form / review the forecasts which can or should process them and which of them should be used to forecast supplied an processed, and to whom and when it should be offered and who should the final process results been requested or processed.

5.6. Determine the length of the forecasting cycle depending on the operational possibilities an way of obtaining market data (e.g. biweekly, monthly, 8-week, quarterly), do not confuse the forecasting cycle with the cycle of operational meetings that verify the operational meetings which can be the element of the forecasting cycle;

5.7. Define the schedule for the forecasting cycle, specifying exactly the dates and responsibilities of individual participants, definitely including key events, the so called *'Consensus Meeting'*.

5.8. Specify the manner of communication in the process and reporting its results,

5.9. Determine the procedure for information exchange with the key areas of the organization (S&OP, PLC, Strategy, specify the annual goal, risk management, etc.)

6. Create the team in charge and select its leader who shall be responsible for this

process and fix him/her within the structures and the organizational hierarchy:

6.1. Diagnose the organization's department which has the most knowledge and is the fastest at obtaining information on the market, trends and changes on that market, the competitive activities, new developments and other phenomena or actions that impact the demand and which allow t swiftly react to changes, in other words a department which is *the closest* to the market, and where the sales forecasting department should be located;

6.2. Present, justify and consult with the top executives:

6.2.1. The requirements regarding the number of the FTEs required within the scope of the number of the FTES (based on previous analysis);

6.2.2. the skills required from team members and leaders (i.e. analytical, communication, leadership skills);

6.2.3. placing the department within the organization's structure;

6.2.4. the challenges which the team will need to face;

6.2.5. the appropriate *fixing* of the team and it leader within the organization's hierarchy;

6.3. conduct recruitment of appropriate persons, best within the organization (who already know the business, market and conditions of the organization) if the human resource are limited, recruit from the outside (best from the industry, the persons who at least know the market).

6.4. present the team and its leaders with the goals, ensure they know the operations procedures and standards;

6.5. sanction the relevance of the process by way of linking indicators of the forecasting quality to the effective incentive system both for the forecasts departments and also any other ones involved in the

process.
7. Together with the forecasting team define the prognostic methods and models and their monitoring procedures:
7.1. select the prognostic methods and models optimal for the individual products (SKU);
7.2. determine optimal parameters for the models based on the available historical data;
7.3. define the procedures for monitoring and optimization of the parameters for the prognostic methods and models.
8. Together with the forecasting team define the forecast quality measurement system:
8.1. Select the error models (types) for the forecast accuracy measurement, optimal for the organization.

8.2. Select the appropriate forecast horizons which will best reflect business costs resulting from forecast errors; tie them to appropriate lead-times in production and supply chain areas.
9. Arrange with the parties concerned the levels, frequency and method of reporting forecast quality.

As it stems from the above, the analytical forecasting area is only a certain part of a complex sales forecasting process. Of key importance to the successful implementation of the forecasting process is the team that should have a good knowledge of the market, products and factors which determine the sales, and also be good at internal communication within the organization.

Process improvement after roll-out

Following implementation of the process a question arises: is it the end of the implementation and development work regarding the sales forecasting process? Such question is clearly rhetorical for at least for two reasons.

First of all, at the time of great market dynamics and technological progress, all business processes must change and over time they require improvements if nothing else in order to face the enormous market competition.

Second of all, which implementing this process at the beginning it is always suggested to use possibly simple methods, methodologies and mathematic models so that all of their users fully understand them and know their strengths and limitation.

One should not worry too much that 'it' could have been done better from the start. It

is only a matter of time, collecting the historical data and experiences, and then using ever more sophisticated methods, models and tools, that the forecast quality may be improved, but still the most spectacular will be the quality improvement obtained at the beginning, after implementing these simplest methods and models.

Upon the implementation there remains much more to do in the area of the process development:
1. Firstly, constant optimization of the forecasting model parameters and interchange of models for the individual products with the more advanced and efficient in terms of quality or adapted to the product life cycle stage – over time each product on the market naturally changes the ales level, course and method.

2. When using some prognostic models a certain forecast quality level is reached, which is hard to exceed, which stems from limitations within the very models; this is when experiments can be started (parallel to one another at an initial stage) with other, more sophisticated models or methods, and following their periodic testing and getting to know them well, replacing the existing ones with them; following the same logic such tools as neural networks may be implemented over time. Apart from good understanding of their operating mechanisms they require a large amount of historical data (minimum 5-7 years).

3. Another element are the tools used to implement the prognostic models; at an initial stage of implementation it is goo to use (many people like and appreciate them) generally available tools which allow to individually implement and improve the prognostic models, such as calculation sheets which apart from the programming options also have many tools embedded for e.g. optimization of the models' parameters; such tools prove effective until a certain moment or with a rather limited product portfolio, and when the number of forecast products is large (one thousand or more), it is warranted to invest in a professional tool supporting forecasting, most frequently integrated with the company's transactional system, databases, CRM systems, Business Intelligence systems, etc.; following implementation of such system, the tools used to date, implemented in a calculation sheet, may act as test tools or tools for review of the models implemented in professional forecasting systems.

4. Another element to support the forecasting process may be implementation of the promotional sales and the NPD management tools, allowing to model the sales executed via a variety of promotions, media support and market launch of new products; support offered by such tools is much appreciated in industries where a significant chunk of sales is generated through promotion or frequent launch of new products.

Additional materials

Additional information and materials that can be used in forecasting workshops can be downloaded from:

HTTPS://SALES4CASTS.COM

Available there are the templates and forecasting spreadsheet models presented in this book as well as other materials and information for developing forecasting competence and workshops